GURNEY
A play by Jon Silkin

Iron Press Drama Editions

First published 1985 by
IRON Press, 5 Marden Terrace
Cullercoats, North Shields
Tyne & Wear NE30 4PD
Tel: Tyneside (091) 2531901

Printed by
Tyneside Free Press Workshop
5 Charlotte Square
Newcastle upon Tyne

Typeset by True North
Book design and paste-up by
Priscilla Eckhard

ISBN 0 906228 23 9

Price £3.50p

Front cover photograph reproduced by kind permission of Haines & Sumner,
of Gloucester

Introduction

'Black Notes' is a phrase from a poem of Gurney's, used as the title of the play in its earlier version. Written to a commission from King's College, Taunton, it was performed on June 4, 1984 – at the School itself, and then at the Brewhouse theatre, Taunton, and The Drum at Plymouth.

Director	*Peter Wood*
Technical direction	*Graeme Delaney*
Music by	*Chris Holmes*
Set design	*Cindy Jones*

This substantially revised version was done in collaboration with Alec Bell, and was first presented by Inckproductions in Dunelm Ballroom, Durham, on November 21, 1984.

Director	*Steve Dearden*
Music by	*John Woolrich*
Design	*Clare Watts*

In the Summer of 1982, I did work for King's College, Taunton, which included a reading of both my poetry and the work of poets of the First World War. In the course of hospitality at King's, Jim Spalding and Peter Wood, both teachers of English at the College, made a proposal that I should write a play based on the life of Ivor Gurney. In the next few months this proposal became, through the generous offices of the Headmaster and Governors, a commission. Work on the first version of the play was, with the assistance of Peter Wood, finished during my residence as Writer at the School during the Michaelmas Term 1983. I was scared by what I had agreed to undertake. However, in late October that year, my wife Lorna Tracy offered to underwrite two weeks at an Artists' "House" in Co. Monaghan, called Annaghmakerrig. She had already spent four weeks in the place and was able to report enthusiastically that 'there was nothing else to do there but eat and write.'

I was fortunate. In the succeeding fortnight of November I managed to draft on pale green and pale lemon coloured paper a substantial part of what became the first two acts, as well as a portion of what became part of the fourth act. During this period, both before and after the stay in Ireland, I read plays, theatre criticism, reviews, theory, listened to Gurney's music, and re-read both his poetry and the biography by Michael Hurd.

What I was attempting, I had worked out, was not a re-creation of Gurney, but a conjunction of lives, a strand of which was modelled on his life, the impulses of which conjunction when fully extended must result in conflict. Gurney did not in fact kill anybody. It was a play about envy, and the ambiguous connections between naivety and innocence. It was concerned with courage and sanity; and towards the finish of the play I made every attempt to present Joseph Gurney's last action in it as the product of his sanity. I may have said too much of what the play is about; but for what Isaac Rosenberg, in a marvellous phrase, called 'the herculean world of ideas', I should mention two works that served to concentrate my thinking. One of these was the brilliant extended essay, *Mozart and Salieri*, by Nadezhda Mandelstam. As soon as I had finished it, I read* Charles Johnston's translation of Pushkin's short verse play with the same title. This period, with its reading, was one of the most exciting in the composition of my work. Nadezhda Mandelstam's essay is concerned with polar impulsions – those of untidy inspiration & creativity and orderly structure – with that, and also with how her husband, Osip Mandelstam, found these two impulsions a necessity reconcileable and consonant – he used a word with musical connotations – with regard to the composition of his poetry. He required both Mozart and Salieri, to write. Pushkin's short drama is about the contrast between these two energies; my own is about the opposition between them. Joseph Gurney's Salieri is his friend and fellow-musician Benjamin Critchley. Benjamin's envy of Joseph Gurney's prodigal talent is fed, painfully fed, by his admiration for it. There is no end to the process of increasing pain and corrosion, the flow of which may only be interrupted, and staunched as a wound is, by his coming to terms with it as much as with the limitations of his nature and its creativity. This he is unable to do. When the natures of these two men are projected they meet in opposition; they work related, not parallel, energies.

I had been given the commission, I believe, partly because of my being a poet, and partly on account of my interest in the writing of the First World War. Ivor Gurney was an individual mauled by the times. Born in the manufacturing and Cathedral city of Gloucester in 1890, the year that his contemporary the poet Isaac Rosenberg was born in Bristol, Gurney's first involvement was with music. Rosenberg's first known poem, 'Ode to David's Harp', was written in 1905, but his energies were at first ostensibly directed towards painting and the visual arts. Through the generosity of three Jewish women, Rosenberg entered the Slade School of Fine Art in 1911. Ivor Gurney, the man *outside* my play, won a Scholarship of £40 a year to the Royal College of Music, and entered it in the Autumn of 1911. In the play, Joseph Gurney complete with Scholarship enrolled in the College in 1914. By 1915 both Ivor and Joseph Gurney were in the Army. Both had volunteered, and been accepted the second go round. Both were gassed, although under different circumstances, both invalided to an Edinburgh hospital where both formed a brief relationship with a Nurse. Thereafter the lives diverge, or rather, the actions within the lives differ.

Ivor Gurney's talent offered a valency for another's envy and predation. That, at least, is my view. In the play that availability is taken up. Joseph Gurney plays Mozart to Benjamin Critchley's Salieri.

Documentary or fiction

I believe that most writers engage this problem some time in their lives as Makers. The closer a writer feels in time, condition, and temperament, to the subject, the more that writer will hesitate to diverge from the apparent facts. But in this crux I was helped by knowing that at least one other writer had already created a documentary drama out of Gurney's fraught life. Nothing would be served by repeating this attempt.

On the other hand, it looked as though it would be interesting if closely associated or related persons were brought into psychological and physical conflict, especially if the mould of their energies bore the pressure of the times. We can always blame the times; they are even more liable to abuse in this respect than are one's parents. But would Joseph Gurney have acted as he did had he not endured infantry experience, or watched others behave as they did when placed in the double position of legalized murderer and paid victim? I do not know what answers may be got by asking these and other questions, but I believe that the necessary questions teazed the trouble out into the open, in such a manner that it could not then be tidied away. I felt that the questions were exemplary especially since our culture seems, increasingly, to find orderliness and propriety preferable to untidiness and creativity. In the play, the musician Stanford sees this last opposition, and asks if such an inevitable clash is more apparent than real. Osip Mandelstam, surely one of the best of the twentieth century Russian poets, believed that such logger-headed situations were neither inevitable nor justified. At least, not in the composition of poetry. But his own extinction, – that hard, joyful and humorous energy made extinct by Stalin, – indicates that the energies represented by Mozart and Salieri are frequently inimical to each other.

The Medium

It is not quite correct to say that I chose verse as the medium for the play. I had read a brief critical work that execrated most of the verse drama from the twentieth century, and I felt that if the form could provide such an opportunity for contumely, even from so jocular and professorial a mind, the form must still contain some of drama's best and most viable energies. But in any event I was not drawn to prose. There was, I believe, never for me a true choice between verse and prose. It was verse or no play. This decision was strengthened by my belief that verse is closer than prose is to speech, and that therefore a flexible, "free", disciplined, variable verse would be not apt so much as the only real expressive means available for the purposes of the play.

I have probably fallen into the error of discussing the content of one's play. Even so, what continues to engage me is how certain arrested energies are released by placing them in unexpected conjunction and relatedness. The destructive individual, and the orderly arrangement of wholesale destruction by regiments of trained men implement

The inward scream, the duty to run mad.

In the last stratum of response by a reader, or an individual member of an audience, no matter how absorbing the ideas, the root of such response must lie in witnessing the conjunction of human beings, or creatures, in relation to one another. A man stroking a cat that stalks off the moment the man has left off his attentions. The hopping sparrow avoiding the hand that desires to feed it. The father's smile for his son, and for his daughter, at different moments in their lives. Joseph Gurney's hardships as well as his egotisms must move one. The ideas will otherwise have little value. I believe in the existence of intellectual passion, but I do believe that its value, the courtesy it does its reader, derive from these animal conjunctions. And I do not by the use of 'animal' wish to imply a simple, simplified delimitation between physical and psychological responses. At any rate, it is the perception of that conjunction which amazes, moves, and sometimes heals, us. We need that today, as much as we ever did.

The people to thank

In the first instance I must thank Jim Spalding and Peter Wood, especially Peter Wood who directed the play, *Black Notes*, as it was called in its earlier form. Peter Wood went carefully through the work, and Lorna Tracy supported me in my periods of dejection, which were frequent. She constantly, early on and throughout its composition, discussed the play with me, and when I felt I dared not, that such and such was not viable, she, out of her experience, mostly assured me it was. All of the Irish period of composition, for instance, was sustained in this way by her – that is, in those crucial initial stages of composition and planning.

The work on the later version of the play, *Gurney*, was done in collaboration – that is not too strong a word – with the Director Alec (Dave) Bell. Alec Bell at first felt the play was not viable, and it was by his working through his own doubts that he was able subsequently to give months of constant, detailed scrutiny and suggestion. Bell was Founder and, for four years, Artistic Director of the Durham Theatre Company now based in Darlington.

I was also helped a great deal by discussions with Peter and Margaret Lewis, and a great deal of valuable professional advice, not to mention insight, on hospital life and routine was given me by Deanna Neville, herself a professional Nurse. She, too, discussed the play and prevented my doubts from tarnishing the process of its composition. My publisher, Pete Mortimer, himself a playwright, also offered detailed criticism, and in the main strongly supported the critical questions asked by Alex Bell. Lastly it gives me pleasure to thank Steve Dearden, the Director of this version of the play, for his quiet determined work with it. In the end, it was such overall collaborative labour that enabled the play to find the form in which it now stands, although its blemishes are all of my own making.

Jon Silkin
Newcastle on Tyne, 1985

Postscript

Readers who have not seen much if any of Gurney's poetry may wonder if I have used any of his verse in the play. There are deliberate quotations from other writers — Isaac Rosenberg, for instance — but to the best of my knowledge there are only two Gurney verse importations: 'blither' and 'Madame, no bon'. Likewise, Gurney's poem, which opens Act 2, scene 4, is not Ivor Gurney's, but an attempt to transpose experience such as a man of Gurney's insight might have appreciated, and to express that in a 'modern' idiom. Again, I should like to say that such an idiom was not intended to be Gurney's. But concerning Gurney's 'modern' idiom, the interested reader may consult my essay Gurney's Voices in *Stand Magazine*, Vol 25, no 4, 1984.

* *Choiseul and Talleyrand* by Charles Johnston, Bodley Head, 1982

Now Israel loved Joseph more than all his children, because he was the son of his old age: and he made him a coat of many colours.

And when his brethren saw that their father loved him more than all his brethren, they hated him, and could not speak peaceably unto him.

Genesis: 37, 3 & 4

And some there be, which have no memorial; who are perished, as though they had never been; and are become as though they had never been born; and their children after them.

Ecclesiasticus: 44,9

GURNEY by Jon Silkin

This play was first performed on Wednesday November 21, 1984 by Inckproductions, at Dunelm House, Durham University. The cast and credits were as follows:

Arthur Sloeman, organist and music teacher	*Jason Blake*
Joseph Gurney	*Chris Murray*
Benjamin Critchley	*Gareth Mills*
Three Schoolboys	*Gordon Fudge*
	David Evans
	Kevin Hosier
Florence Gurney, Joseph's mother	*Andy Nixon*
Betty Bisely	*Liz Barnes*
Canon Cheesman	*Kevin Williamson*
Charles Stanford, Professor of the Royal College of Music	*James Breen*
Elizabeth	*Sorrel Oates*
Ironmask, a Private	*Tom Stevenson*
Handshone, a Private	*Henry Whitcomb*
Fly, drudge to Corporal	*Patrick Martin*
Corporal Snatcher	*Gordon Fudge*
Other Soldier	*David Evans*
Adjutant	*Rory Morrison*
Germans	*Kevin Hosier*
	Joe Hawes
Mary, student at the Academy	*Kate Hampshire*
Jenny Hawthornden, a Nurse	*Jackie Robinson*
Doctors	*Jason Blake*
	Henry Whitcomb
Two Orderlies	*Camilla Shand*
	Patrick Martin
Warden of Asylum	*Joe Hawes*
Waiter	*Kevin Hosier*
Waitress	*Diana Hare*

Director	*STEVE DEARDEN*
Setting	*CLARE WATTS*
Costume	*MARTHA WANSBROUGH*
Lighting	*FARZIN GHANDCHI*
Producer	*TOBY MACDONALD*
with	*LOUISE BATES*
	MARGARET RAMSAY
	JACKIE ROBINSON
	ELAINE WHEELER
Make-Up	*CHRIS RUTHVEN*
	JANE BROOKER
	ANNA SHONE
Music	*JOHN WOOLRICH*
Musical Director and Piano	*JOHN YOUNG*
Clarinet	*LIZ EVERETT*
Violin	*NANCY LLOYD*
Tapes made and operated by	*STEVE MOORE*

GURNEY

ACT 1

Scene 1: *A house in Barton Street, Gloucester 1914.*

Joseph sits slumped and lanky in a wheelback chair in the corner of a room – one of the few areas remaining to the family after the tailoring business has taken over so much of the house. He suffers from indigestion which from time to time he indicates. The room in which Joseph sits, still yet poised, as if waiting for some occurence, is the ground-floor back room, in front of which is the shop. The front-door bell of this can be heard to give a single clang, as if in modest imitation of the city's cathedral bell. Joseph remains seated.

Florence Gurney, Joseph's mother, enters, looks at her son (still) in the chair, looks away with cold aggression. Then her face lights up as she starts to speak. She glances frequently at her son – as if scolding him.

FLORENCE   Mother could sing very nicely she was always singing Scotch songs and English, Irish and Welsh, Father was alto in the Bisley Choir but he didn't sing at home like Mother did my dear old Grandfather and his brother uncle Robert he was a Batchelor and Mother said he nursed his Mother till she died and wouldn't let anybody else do a thing for her her arm chair was covered with white dimity and he used to wash everything himself after he had dug the garden the spade and the fork and all the diggers were shone like silver and put down in the cellar and the white stones which showed up through the dirt was scrubbed white...

During the mention of 'shone like silver' one hears the voice of Joseph, the boy soprano, singing the hymn (277) 'The day thou gavest, Lord, is ended'; his voice aspires like a bird, lifting up its sweetness and power.

     he would give us some flowers if we wouldn't put them on the graves that was popery well I wish I knew where they came from they were not the regular sort of Bisley people they had too much in them... that's so, isn't it Joseph?

     (Joseph does not answer. With a shrug of impatience and contempt she turns from him and continues)

     Grandfather was a good man the Luggs round Stroud are the most respected of anybody and you can say what you like a good ancestor is something to be proud of but Joseph hasn't seen a lot of the Luggs he knew the Gurneys better and they hadn't a note of music in them...

     (turns to Joseph)

Joseph. Joseph, you fool. How will the business fare,
if you sit like a white stone? Not as clean, I daresay.
Sing, or get to work.

(Joseph sits and says nothing. She exits to the front shop. Slowly Joesph gets up.)

JOSEPH   That's what she thinks of me. I was a boy soprano,
and once I sang for a singer who got drunk; it was in dockland,
and she got pissed. Then she begged me
to sing for her. I did so,
my voice sweet as a parsnip.   My first
public music. Now what?

Act 1, scene 2

A meadow on the fringes of Gloucester, from which the Cathedral can be seen. Extending forward from that, a pool of shimmering gently wrinkled water — a small basin formed from the muddy liquid of the Severn. A fence of slatted horizontals held by poles halved vertically holds these in parallel and in series, the whole fence coming up from the water's edge. Chilly autumn day 1914, the sun gold, as if the combustion required to burn the particles of cold into light gave it a foggy tinge. Joseph and Benjamin. In Act 1, scene 2, the intercutting occurs between the two "geographies" of Sloeman's teaching room, and the Dockland. These intercuttings are marked with asterisks. The two Geographies are on stage at the same time.

BENJAMIN   Do you always talk of music?

JOSEPH   I do, for Gloucester's sake. I love its railways,
the Glosters, regiment of enlisted men,
its four roads of Rome lashed into a cross;
and the squared-off Cathedral, rising vertically
from that set of four squares. Also,
the muddy river and docklands. If I lost this
I'd lose everything.

BENJAMIN   You don't belong
to the docklands.

JOSEPH   I'd like to belong to the hills,
to what music people make, as they set
their ploughs to. Or I'd be a lock-keeper.
I'll work with my hands, if I can't write.

BENJAMIN	You could. I want to write
	for my livelihood; to be musicianly, held together
	by what Dr. Sloeman calls structure. You don't like
	Sloeman. *pause*
JOSEPH	It's like a steam engine: I prefer
	its pure energy, its mischief.

*   *   *

Dr. Sloeman's house is close by the Cathedral. The man is organist to the Church and he also teaches music to students many of whom owe to him the fundaments of their musical education. These would include Critchley and Joseph who have been studying with him for a number of years, and who are shortly to take the scholarship exam for the Royal College of Music. This is an important time for them and for Arthur Sloeman. The birds will fly now or not at all and he may be excused for thinking that only one of them is about to be fledged. For him authenticity lies in craftsmanship and execution. This is just. Less happily, he is concerned to have his aesthetic judgements vindicated. Gloucester has a share of the Three Choirs Festival and nothing untidy, uncraftsmanly and so, inauthentic, should leave his door for the academy's. Sloeman is not an unjust man, nor a cruel one, but he rejects inspiration on three accounts. First, his own capacities rarely if at all include that operation and he cannot therefore believe highly enough in any pupil of his who has inspiration – or else one would not be his pupil. With less scrupulousness, Sloeman does not really value inspiration for the same want in his own composition. He is musicianly, admirable in his response to the demands of craft and the constant practice needed to maintain skill; and he knows that much of both is required for composition and performance. But Sloeman also suspects inspiration to be bogus, and accounts for the palpable artists by indicating their magnificent competence. He is not an unkind man and in many ways a valuable musician, but he would fumble if asked to name his deficiencies.

Benjamin is playing exercises on the violin. It is autumn 1914. Remains of a burnt-through fire powder a small elegant grate.

SLOEMAN	There is a kind of prose
	virtue to your playing. It will do.
	It will do and you will pass; the poetry
	we leave to others.

Which others?

BENJAMIN	
SLOEMAN	You would not have me be invidious.

(Dr Sloeman is sweating lightly. He pats his forehead.)

JOSEPH	Sir, I am going to play with a rod of iron today.
SLOEMAN	You do, often. With a rod of iron.

(Joseph plays, not too well; but he is trying, and from him certain phrases emerge that have genuine passion and execution although less polish than Benjamin's.)

SLOEMAN	Enough, that is enough. Gurney, if you are to pass you will be needing tact and accuracy.
JOSEPH	Is that all?
SLOEMAN	It is enough.

(Joseph sniggers)

SLOEMAN	You need not think, Gurney, that your payments are purchase-money for rudeness. Or unkindness.
JOSEPH	I am sorry, sir, I meant no unkindness.

(Benjamin manufactures a snort)

SLOEMAN	Go on then, Gurney. Try it again.

(Joseph does, but it is not better. The same wild playing, sometimes with authentic passion, sometimes with carelessness. Joseph's execution conforms to Sloeman's earlier estimate – 'it lacks structural drive'. The judgment is fair. Sloeman signals to him to stop.)

*   *   *

JOSEPH	I hope we study together, and win that scholarship. Would you work in London?
BENJAMIN	*(thoughtfully)*
	Possibly. *pause* I'd like to hear music well-made I want the elegant waistcoat of people's attention.
JOSEPH	Which they don't wear here?
BENJAMIN	I'm sharing honesty, which we've always shared, even your mother's cold shouts. We're like the male violet, two different petals attached to a stem.

JOSEPH	I shall always care for you. When I publish my first songs – if I do – you shall have their dedication.

*   *   *

BENJAMIN	Is competence the whole thing, sir?
SLOEMAN	Nearly all. Wanting it, the music cannot struggle through, gets clogged, or, as they say up north, clagged. It is distorted by incompetence. I do not mean, Gurney, that you are so, but you are careless. That is not music which you play out of an excess of feeling.
JOSEPH	It is not excess, sir, it is my feelings.
BENJAMIN	But he means first the playing must make its grade or the music will not reach its listener. Though I know, without feeling there is little music.
JOSEPH	Are you sure? Show me.

(Benjamin plays with exquisite sensitivity and tact – his best so far this day.)

JOSEPH	But that is with love, that is what music should be. I ought to play like that, I know. And I will.
BENJAMIN	With inspiration you make feeling your competence, – it is a fine, sensitive creature, nostrils dilating lightly, breath measured and sweet.
SLOEMAN	That's enough of aesthetics, Benjamin, even from you. Gurney, please, try again. And imagine me your invigilator.

JOSEPH   That is what you are.

          (He plays and it is better.)

                    *   *   *

BENJAMIN   But the war,
          and its needs. Will you enlist now?

JOSEPH   I want to serve my land.

BENJAMIN   Country?

          (enacts thrust of bayonet with a stick lying about)

JOSEPH   – so if
          my stomach-trouble permits me
          – look, this is for what –

          (he stoops and picks up a pinch of soil)

BENJAMIN   *(bursts out laughing)*

          For mud

JOSEPH   When the rains rain
          the dead turn into that, they rot. But this land
          is precious

BENJAMIN   but also
          the people on it, who we love

JOSEPH   I love music.

                    *   *   *

SLOEMAN   Isn't it sufficient
          you bring the fine tact of craft
          and thread your music with it? Is anything
          wrong with such sensitivity?

JOSEPH   I try.
          I can't do better.
          I thank you for requiring it
          from me – as if I had sensitivity.
          What I do is my best. And I believe, sir,
          that love is the first and last thing

SLOEMAN	it is the last thing, though even to love a girl requires skills – the filaments of love
JOSEPH	do you know about love, sir?
SLOEMAN	Do you?
BENJAMIN	In fairness, nor do I sir. But we both will, and Joseph's acts of love – sir...of the creating Word – our solemn medal of investment in Christ, which, sir, we turn over, and there's only blank – sir, we share devotion; even Gloucester's heated congregation has its forms of love.
SLOEMAN	Pretty speech, which, however, I don't despise; the three choirs serving England, with that queer bloke, Elgar, his discordant pernickety grandeur. Yes, we love the Love, probably.

*   *   *

JOSEPH	I think I've loved myself, first. And the curate's kindness – him – at least. And Miss Betty, who gives me tea after I've played duo –
BENJAMIN	isn't that what we join up for?
JOSEPH	I'd like to walk by the canal.

Fade. When it lights again they are by the canal in Dockland. Unlike the city which has an ornate pinched dignity at its centre, but like the Cathedral in its being well-built, the warehouses are squarely constructed. The sense of water allows the mind egress, and offers an idea of distance that relieves what some might find parochial and closed. This clumsy vigour is ungentle, and despite its strength has a touch of envy, as if the labour imposed upon those who work or live by the docks vies with their health.

BENJAMIN	I like this dockland, the large blanked-out windows, the warehouses turned in on their riches
JOSEPH	like burghers.
BENJAMIN	The neat cut of them, their fastidious construction. When men exhaust, these still house their goods.

JOSEPH	Even more – you like them – than the Severn?
BENJAMIN	I want to become Salieri: the precise life. And you can be Schubert.
JOSEPH	I am he; I write I eat, when I do, like him. I eat a huge creamy bun stuck with a cherry. My songs are mine but he's lent me his mind, to write like him.
BENJAMIN	If you had the mind to. I shall write like Salieri: precise, fitted, as the wood of a cross fits. If I were the wood of the cross, I'd be sure to hold the Christ, firmly, regardless of the agony; I would hold the man on the cross till he dropped. Like a child surfeited. He would be my fruit.

BENJAMIN *(looks around and notices young men of their age approaching)*

Joseph, do you know what;
some of our young scholars approach.

JOSEPH	who? must we see them?
BENJAMIN	Apostles of learning: look for yourself – like us, trained to nothing

(enter three young men)

FIRST	So? you work here?
SECOND	slummin'?
FIRST	What, batty Gurney, the tailor's wife? He'd never slum.

(One of them pokes Gurney's stomach with his forefinger, then tries to reach his balls.)

THIRD	*(to Benjamin)* Critchley, don't you teach him nothing? what? what?

(Benjamin remains silent)

FIRST   not going to say nothing – neither
of you?

THIRD   Not a thing. We could learn you a few "items".
What's batty Gurney got
in his pants? Scullions? No bigger than, I bet.
Let's have a peek.

JOSEPH   No.

THIRD   Do you hear?
No, he says. A lot of trouble
in a little water

FIRST   he "declines" the kind offer. Wait, Gurney,
the army may get you

SECOND   if
it takes him.

THIRD   Unless he wangles his ticket.
Wink wink. *pause*   Some one is
certain to have him.

(they all laugh)

THIRD   Here, Critchley.

(Benjamin does not reply)

                                    I said, Critchley.
You ain't no manners, have you? None
whatsoever. It's a bleedin' shame, because
we don't want to be the ones to teach you. But we will,
if the lord puts his word in. Got any
hairs on your cock, Gurney?

JOSEPH   Yes.

(Joseph lunges, and the fight starts. The three crowd round him, and eventually beat him up. Then they turn his shirt back-to-front and tie the arms behind him in the form of a primitive strait-jacket.)

THIRD   Laugh, Critchley; this ain't no funeral.

(Benjamin erupts into wild laughter, and even the three young men stare at him. Gurney struggles with his confinement, but the three boys hold him. Benjamin is still laughing as they move off. As they go, one of them spits in Benjamin's face.)

21

SECOND   Yer slime, not a friend.

                          *   *   *

SLOEMAN   Gurney, if you pass
                it will be miraculous
                like threading hemp through a needle's eye.

BENJAMIN   Well Joseph, less hemp and more strings. Now –
                two three four

                (they play in uneasy but jocular unison)

                less hemp and more flax

                (Benjamin breaks into laughter and Joseph follows him)

Act 1, scene 3

The time of year is October, 1914. We feel some gleam of light off the clerestory windows through the open door. Betty, an older, musical friend and companion of Joseph's is preparing the table on which the celebration foods are being laid. She works quickly, deftly, quietly, adding touches that will ensure the pleasure of those to come. She smiles as she works. The room is Sloeman's, in the Cathedral, where Joseph and Benjamin have been taught; fitting place, one would suppose, for such a celebration to mark their both gaining scholarships to the Royal College of Music in London. Such a double success should please all those who are to arrive. She works in silence, mostly, but sometimes she hums some music which she has been playing, as may be shown by her stopping to strum a passage on the table. Then she returns to setting things in order. Canon Cheesman, Joseph's godfather, and friend, enters. They smile at each other, but say nothing. Cheesman gently, and at a distance, follows her around, but does not actually help. Eventually she stops, straightens up, smiles.

BETTY   There, that should do it.

                (She smiles and then exits)

Cheesman looks round surveying the "comestibles". It is a fine feast. It is, in fact, a feast. Old-fashioned and luxurious by virtue of that generosity produced by those who cannot properly afford it, but who, in concert with others, produce the necessary that will ensure pleasure. It will. Cheesman, who is sedate, and gentle, but not bumbling, stares at the decanter of wine for some time. Then, making a movement to straighten his collar, but thinking it not necessary, goes to the decanter of wine, and pours a nip into a glass. He drinks with modest satisfaction until Joseph enters quietly, and who, perceiving his friend drinking, comes up and puts a hand on his shoulder.

This both startles and then embarrasses Cheesman. After a moment both laugh. Then Cheesman puts down his drink and makes to straighten Joseph's tie, which needs this attention. Joseph nimbly avoids him. Eventually this dumb play is broken.

JOSEPH   Does mother love me?

           (Cheesman does not answer)

           why is she so cold?
           I used to think it normal to be cold. Is it normal
           to write music? Then why
           do none of us do it, but me?

CHEESMAN   Dr. Sloeman does.

JOSEPH   Such music, I wouldn't want it sung to me dead.

CHEESMAN   Your friend
           Benjamin.

JOSEPH   Why isn't he batty? or perhaps
           he is. No, I wouldn't want them to call him
           batty.

CHEESMAN   He is not, you aren't.
           But you are the best maker in Gloucester.

JOSEPH   Perhaps.
           Ten months ago I was seventeen. There is music in me still,
           thank God.

CHEESMAN   And do you know, your voice improves still?
           So you see you need not fear, Joseph, that I, your godfather,
           shall violate your mother's care,
           her dear and precious care. Her's is the first offering.

JOSEPH   I know. And have, for many years, Michael.

CHEESMAN   Yes,
           now you are old enough to call me that, and others
           need not mind, or smile, as they used
           when we walked arm in arm.

JOSEPH   What harm was there
           in that?

CHEESMAN   None. But keep your humour no matter how
           bedraggled the life. My father, on a ship,
           for some offence, I don't know what, they flogged him
           to death.

JOSEPH	*(not really interested)* Why?
CHEESMAN	It was original sin. Only the human delights to hurt.
JOSEPH	Your master, the Vicar, says original sin can't be erased.
CHEESMAN	Perhaps my master is wrong.
JOSEPH	That's what I want, to live without sin. If I can create music – when the sun goes down the other side of the railway, a happier hot disc, it's rosy, powerful, filled with created heat.

(There is a sound of footsteps and Florence Gurney arrives with Betty, a musician who has helped Joseph considerably.)

FLORENCE	*(to Betty)* This is the root of it, I'm sure. Joseph has done well, but goodness, how much better he could have.

Silence

BETTY	Joseph, we do congratulate you. Mrs. Gurney, so few from here get to College, though we've music of sorts
FLORENCE	good music. My people made it, the best of the Parish, though the Gurneys – never had a stitch of music. If they sang, they choked.
BETTY	Though if we sing it sounds well enough. Joseph has done fine.
FLORENCE	And better still is my motto.
CHEESMAN	It is – for us all. He will grow, he loves what he makes.
FLORENCE	Nothing very much, he loves. He loves his wheelback chair in which he's inclined to slouch, aren't you, Joseph?

CHEESMAN   Any two fools can make a child, Mrs. Gurney.

FLORENCE   Indeed, Canon. How would you know?

CHEESMAN   it takes
             a craftsman to make a chair.
             Joseph loves his craft.

             (Enter Dr. Sloeman: he perceives that Joseph is about to pour the
             celebratory wine and is clearly displeased at this.)

SLOEMAN   I don't believe
             we should drink yet.

JOSEPH   Sir, why is that?

SLOEMAN   Because
             the main person, apart from you,
             the celebrant in whose success,
             whose slant light we stand in, is not here.

CHEESMAN   *(Interrupting Joseph)*

             Just so.

JOSEPH   But let me put out
             the wine.

SLOEMAN   You shall not pour it yet.

JOSEPH   Not pour?

FLORENCE   Not pour, not drink. Do as he says,
             you are rude otherwise, Joseph

SLOEMAN   Not rudeness,
             disregard, rather, for his friend; in whose success
             Joseph follows, learns, succeeds.

JOSEPH   Sir, I admit his gift, I always have.
             Who are you to tell me I do not?

CHEESMAN   *(guilelessly)*   Is there harm
             in the wine?

BETTY   Innocent, Michael, and pure;
             but it should wait
             to celebrate your friend's friend.

FLORENCE   This is a pleasant room.
             I love the Cathedral, the sun
             dissolving through glass.

SLOEMAN   You are a seamstress
                  Mrs. Gurney?

FLORENCE   A tailor, Dr. Sloeman, for such as you
                  and many like you.
                                    All men must fit the crutch
                  and the tape-measure; all, the scissors hands.

SLOEMAN   Not all men fit.

FLORENCE   It's the musician speaks,
                  the fire's voice, in which we heat, I know.
                  But the tailor cuts the cloth
                  so the man must fit it.

JOSEPH   I'd rather be a lock-keeper,
                  letting the water pour through

CHEESMAN   we cut the cloth,
                  Mrs. Gurney, to fit the man.

JOSEPH   I'd prefer it. You know what? I'd open
                  the lock-gates, with a pipe between my teeth.
                  Water and tobacco, and the garlic flowers stinking the sheet
                  of air, by running water. I'd prefer it
                  to music's calculations.

SLOEMAN   The calculations
                  are never passionate.
                  Water is not
                  its calculation, its pure intent.
                  That's what you can never learn.

BETTY   Dr., this is a celebration

SLOEMAN   You are right,
                  Miss Bisley, as you have always thought you were
                  about your pupil.

BETTY   Doctor,
                  we are here to celebrate, and pay you tribute
                  for your students. You taught them
                  music's instincts, not awry, but upright.
                  Like a tower at a crossroads, the great Church,
                  windows dripping music, because music
                  is the first instinct.

SLOEMAN	Yes, Madam. If music is an instinct —
	(to Joseph)
	Then whose truth is it? — yours or your friend's?
JOSEPH	Benjamin has some truth, sir; I work
	with mine.
FLORENCE	Not Joseph, Doctor, he don't work,
	not as he should. The Luggs were hard workers;
	the name tells all, except their voices' sweetness.
	That was nothing to do with the name.
BETTY	Mrs. Gurney
	I should like to ask
FLORENCE	yes
BETTY	if ever Joseph
	has fitted your cloth.
FLORENCE	No, never
BETTY	if he has ever once
JOSEPH	I sang once
	for a drunken friend of yours, an opera singer,
FLORENCE	She was
	never my friend
JOSEPH	and I did it well
FLORENCE	not
	your place to say,
	though you outshine cathedral glass.
SLOEMAN	He
	needs no encouragement, Mrs. Gurney.
	pause
FLORENCE	No, Doctor. Only work makes us what we are,
	Gloucestershire work,
	down in the market where the trade is; you wouldn't know.
SLOEMAN	I know, and don't like it.
FLORENCE	You know, and don't have to.

(She pours herself some wine and spills it. Joseph takes the decanter from her, roughly after all and in embarrassment, and despite Sloeman's remonstrating with him, pours for everyone. Sloeman

27

refuses his glass and Joseph pours one and leaves it on the table beside him.)

JOSEPH   What have I ever done of anything
that's ever pleased you, like water
that would chafe continuously, chafe and flow,
mother, from one end
of earth to the other?
I'm glad to be leaving; there was never anything here
for me.

FLORENCE   You are right;
more Gurney than Lugg

JOSEPH   More music than misery.

SLOEMAN   What of it? There must always be
misery, where music is made.

JOSEPH   Sir,
it is a joy.

SLOEMAN   Sir – it is afterwards,
if ever.

JOSEPH   What are you telling me now?

(Sloeman knocks over his glass, which breaks)

shouts

SLOEMAN   That's what you make me do. I told you
I wanted to wait.

(to Joseph)

You know, the war is here; who
will pay for that?

JOSEPH   *(very quietly)*

You mean
who is to get themselves killed?

SLOEMAN   Thousands
will.

JOSEPH   Me amongst them?

pause   (with insolence and aggression)

Is that what you want, – *Sir?*

pause

I'm afraid not.

SLOEMAN The best fellows go.

FLORENCE Who are the best men,
Doctor; what age, what shape
have they?

SLOEMAN I would go.

FLORENCE Then go.

CHEESMAN Mrs. Gurney
there is no war here.

FLORENCE There is
with him and me. For to despite me,
my family of Luggs from which I came,
bare like a flower, like a prim violet,
– he picks on my son.

SLOEMAN I said your son is one of many
one worthy of the sacrifice.

FLORENCE We know
what you mean, and it is not good.
You judge well, but your heart's mean fire
reduces to ash; a quarry perpetually
of others' lives, which you scoop out, –
of use to congratulate yourself.

pause

I know it, your pupils is your success
never matter how much it's their own strength
fastens them to their talent, to produce songs,
like Joseph has. Better a proud mother,
than a teacher's pride.

SLOEMAN Pride
given for one's land. The truth, Mrs. Gurney,
is crooked. I care for my craft
and care for who care to have it,
to tread delicately over the earth. Joseph
loves, but he tramples. Never could I,
in my judgment, have given him his scholarship.

I was astounded when he got it.

JOSEPH   I've no music
in me? are you telling me that?

FLORENCE   So you have took
my cash and his work, these years,
for nothing?

SLOEMAN   To be frank, Ma'am, not
for nothing.

*(A long silence. It is as long as the audience, and the actors, can bear.
It should also be an ambiguous one, as if the acted situation had
become a real one in which, because of the stress, they had forgotten
their parts, and their tongues. Outside, a melancholy military band
can be heard, not loud, playing a hymn. 'The day thou gavest, Lord,
is ended'. It finishes in mid-tune and never continues.)*

BETTY   You drive wedges between each of us, Sloeman.

*(Enter Benjamin who, though late, arrives with composure and with
a certain controlled excitement. Sloeman seems momentarily
startled, then walks over to him and embraces him. This is clearly
generous, although not something he often does.)*

SLOEMAN   Benjamin, I am so glad. Of both pupils
you are each the best.

BENJAMIN   Sir, your refined
attention served us.

SLOEMAN   It is talent,
application, the huge shaped metal. I love you
for it – both of you.

BETTY   And I. It's a sweet time for us

CHEESMAN   and I,
who think Gloucester makes of London a wide street,
a fuller street – London will hear
a new sound

SLOEMAN   childish vision,
but a pleasing one.

CHEESMAN   It pleases God,
perhaps.

SLOEMAN	You, as priest, are I know in direct communication. Tongues of angels and choirboys.
JOSEPH	*(aside to Sloeman)* All of our friends came for this, sir, which should have been a good time.
BENJAMIN	You'll make it good, Joseph. At the College you'll remove the clutter from their rooms, and will fill them gently with your music.
JOSEPH	Sounds indecent.
BENJAMIN	Me; I'm going into the Army.
SLOEMAN	*(to Joseph)* You'll work everything out in your music. *brief pause* *(to Benjamin)* What?
BENJAMIN	There is war over Europe. Berlin says it, Paris, Moscow, – the archduke's splintered brain. And London. The mild English hear the mell of war.
JOSEPH	And me? must we all join?
BENJAMIN	You? Stiffen your senses, whatever stings, you, make music of it.
JOSEPH	That's nothing. And it feels as if music is dead. England demands service, that's what you say. The mean dockland, the meaner warehouses stuffed with riches never sampled by us.
BENJAMIN	Whose riches? They're all inside you. *pause* I'll be a band-boy, a grenadier.
FLORENCE	*(to Joseph)* You're not going to join, you're not fit to.

JOSEPH	Mother
	let me breathe.
BETTY	And if Benjamin goes –
	but he mustn't. This is stupid. There's no war,
	only murder. A hinge opening
	into death – leave
	the war, go to college.
JOSEPH	All the men
	of Gloucester will be on the road,
	for the recruiting office
CHEESMAN	There's only
	one of you
BETTY	the college chose two to make a pair,
	and both of you for music
JOSEPH	if they get killed,
	those men I'm one of
SLOEMAN	Oh, you could be; sturdy
	like a young horse, with rifle and pack
	strapped to you, though not the great arms
	of a limber. You'll do.
JOSEPH	I would.
BENJAMIN	I think my scholarship will be this war
CHEESMAN	You could wait for the war to call you.
SLOEMAN	What, Cheesman?
	Offer up to your country, with mechanical body,
	not your own will?
FLORENCE	*(goes as if to strike him)*
	I've lost patience. You're meddlesome,
	stuffed with mischief
SLOEMAN	Your care, Mrs. Gurney, is
	for your son, for you. This is the perfect time – of war;
	the double coin of you and she – of purification
	of the old tribe, England.
FLORENCE	A shame, a blotch
	on your music. I shouldn't wonder all the care
	in the world perishes, for the likes of you.
	I drink my son's health, his gift,
	quicker nor yours, Ben Critchley.

BENJAMIN	Quite right, Mrs. Gurney, except for the courage.
JOSEPH	There's a swelling in my neck, my breath – everything comes tightly –

pause

CHEESMAN	Can I help? please
JOSEPH	if I had less cold gulping my breath – my blood is altering
BETTY	Joseph, my friend, what is it?

(she rushes over to him)

JOSEPH	My senses are snowy...as if frozen gas – I feel stiff and still as if love were a malady, and no love like packed snow.... look at me, Benjamin, with your face of War. Mother, touch me. Put your hands on me.

(He begins to tremble, then goes rigid. He is having an ideographic, that is, an emotion-based, fit.)

Act 2, scene 1

Elizabeth's office. Her living quarters are also in the College, though off-stage, and this living-in spills into her office which thus contains touches of her life. An interesting vase which itself holds the flowers, small and almost spikey, of winter jasmine. There are some books, including contemporary poets. W. B. Yeats, and a volume of Swinburne's. Also a prose book by Edward Thomas. College Archivist and College Secretary, Elizabeth is also a product of the RCM. She is writing. Silence. Then bursts of singing, mingled with the brassy instruments practising, noise such as one only hears in a music school. Then silence again. She gets up, goes to consult a small filing drawer, touches the flowers with her finger-tips, and then stands quietly, serious and vulnerable. There is a knock; her posture alters. A pause and then Charles Stanford, doyen of music teachers, composer and musicologist, enters. He is clearly glad to see Elizabeth, and she him.

STANFORD	I have a question on Vivaldi.
ELIZABETH	I've many, all unanswered.

STANFORD	I shall start again.
ELIZABETH	*(shyly)* Do.
STANFORD	Vivaldi
ELIZABETH	Vivaldi, Antonio – born, question-mark; but death in 1741. For certain. Neither date nor place of birth known. For certain. Patient searching of archives –Venice churches, for instance,– has yielded, nothing at all. Although, even if Vivaldi was not Venetian-born
STANFORD	halt
ELIZABETH	even so, born somewhere within that rich eastern Republic. Taught violin by his patient father *(stops)*
STANFORD	as archivist
ELIZABETH	as ex-student
STANFORD	Elizabeth, I shall be forced to insist
ELIZABETH	also: College secretary, Matron of students' ghostly endeavours
STANFORD	archivist, I say. *pause* What's more I need information, precise and detailed, on the scoring of the fourth of Vivaldi's 'Seasons'.
ELIZABETH	Yes, sir.
STANFORD	And whether Count *(during this last she has risen and gone to her filing drawer)*
ELIZABETH	Wenceslas of Marzin
STANFORD	yes; very fine. And if the musical detail, as propounded in letters to the Count, corresponded to the music he wrote for him
ELIZABETH	or if making such explanations to him forced on Vivaldi changes

STANFORD   *(almost together)*
AND   in the composition.
ELIZABETH
                                        pause
                                   Laughter.

STANFORD   Yes.

ELIZABETH   Then, Sir Charles,
               why not say so at the start?

STANFORD   Ma'am,
               you are provoking me.

ELIZABETH   Sir, you have
               me provoked, already.   *pause*   Sir Charles,
               I produce the goods. Always.

STANFORD   As you say,
               Elizabeth; always.   *pause*
               And you will search these questions out?

ELIZABETH   Yes,
               sir.

               (she goes again to the filing-drawer)

STANFORD   And also

ELIZABETH   non solum
               sed etiam

STANFORD   I require more information

ELIZABETH   more?

STANFORD   on
               a student.   *pause*   Benjamin Critchley.   *pause*

ELIZABETH   Who he?   *pause*
               No sir, I know who he is;
               friend of Gurney's. Though sir, of the two

STANFORD   No!
               of the two?

ELIZABETH   *(slightly embarrassed)*
                         Gurney's

STANFORD   the more untidy

ELIZABETH	I was about to say
STANFORD	chaotic, indeed his manuscripts of composition are, at times, inchoate. But Critchley
ELIZABETH	I would have said the less talented. And Gurney the more
STANFORD	*(scrutinizing her)* you would have. The conduct of genius. The ploys of a musical ruffian
ELIZABETH	what is a musical ruffian, Sir Charles? I have never seen one
STANFORD	You see one.
ELIZABETH	Where? *pause*
STANFORD	Ma'am?
ELIZABETH	Sir?
STANFORD	*(smiling)* He is very good. *pause* You do know. It is Gurney. They say, in demeanour, who know of it, in musical demeanour, he resembles the soft shaded melancholy of that quick trout, Schubert.
ELIZABETH	Yes sir. *pause* *More seriously* His music is soft, shaded, melancholy. *(with quiet warmth)* Well done. *(Stanford looks up, almost shyly, under her approbation)*
ELIZABETH	Sir Charles, I care for you – we all do. We support your spikey authoritarian... because you're generous, that's why. In that: item, you suffer fools, not at all; you suffer other's talent, as if greater than yours; and if it should be, and if it is, you suffer that divine burden, with grace, passion, generosity. Which is a great deal.

A knock. Joseph enters immediately, wearing his thick dark-blue Severn pilot's coat.

STANFORD It is too much.   *pause*
You will let me have that Vivaldi matter and...*(exchange of understanding glances)*

(Exit Stanford)

ELIZABETH Yes, come in.

JOSEPH I have written five *Elizabethan* songs,
it is Fletcher's words – the music is his, too,
but he took me by the arm, showed me, gently,
where the music lay beneath a stone, its sharp
damp leafy skeleton. I fleshed it
with my music – interleaving the words, as if
they were never sung before; the two formed
music, I mean, what the voice sings,
and the piano strums. Will you hear them?

ELIZABETH   In your time,
in this college many will, if they're good.   *pause*
I should like to.

JOSEPH   Oh, to be well.
I wish I were.

ELIZABETH   What is the matter?

JOSEPH   If only
this atrocious nervousness would pass,
the serpent that works in me. The trail
of the dyspeptic creature is over me still.
Do you understand? I wish
I had a cavity where men stuff their guts.

ELIZABETH But I do understand, and sympathize.

JOSEPH   Elizabeth –
May I call you that?

ELIZABETH   Yes.

JOSEPH You know, my mother is cold. It's not adult
to blame my parent for my life; but my life
is what it is, and she, what she is.
Sometimes my senses ache
like snow, I am white, no man's flesh.
I cannot think then, can't work

37

the complicated patch of other's words
with my music. For it is mine, my tongue that speaks
with a voice, not its own: angel's voice, soprano.
If I can't compose
I feel in torment.

ELIZABETH   Then you can feel.

JOSEPH   I feel
something terrible approaching

ELIZABETH   and you need to talk to me?

JOSEPH   if only I could.

ELIZABETH   If only you would
manage to.

JOSEPH   What do you mean?

ELIZABETH   Don't you know?   *pause*
it is about silk, the stockinged material   *pause*
the weave of one material made cross-ply
by two voices upon each other.

JOSEPH   What do these voices mean?

ELIZABETH   Guess.

JOSEPH   Lucky them. More than me
to be...strong as the weave of silk is.
I envy the work of the lock-keeper; he opens
the doors and the water floods through his doing,
a gift of strength and tact. Tactful with the water
then the boat comes, the barge with a man and his pipe,
his dog

ELIZABETH   *(shyly)*
              his wife.

JOSEPH   Today, I had a letter from Miss Betty;
she recommends the army. The safest place, she says,
for a man of music and nerves. Do you
believe her?

ELIZABETH   I'm not demanding you enlist,
if that's what you mean.

38

JOSEPH	I tried, once, and failed, once. It's the being asked as if one were afraid. I was afraid. And also the flag of many colours, the standard, was severely fluttered; I became the colours all hot for war. And then wilted as if the breeze no longer insisted. It's the being forced to go, bashed with white feathers, that I hate.
ELIZABETH	It's all we women have.
JOSEPH	It's not. You have our feelings in your hands, you stroke us until we grow, you caress us, and then stop.
ELIZABETH	Have I stopped?
JOSEPH	I look at you steadily, breathe in, and say, No, you have not. *pause* I'm frightened to say it – I might love you.
ELIZABETH	I do love you

silence

and I've felt your care for me.   *pause*
If your need is tender care, your need
is stronger than your care.

JOSEPH	So?
ELIZABETH	If it is so, then since need is strongest in you, you shall have that of me. The strongest need, the strongest supply of love a woman – that I – can give. Nothing is bought, Joseph, but I will give you it.
JOSEPH	*(coming close)* Will you kiss me once?
ELIZABETH	*(she kisses him, very slowly and several times)* Then let me hear your music, and hear your voice in mine as the lining of the thickness in milk, that of smooth cloth in a man's jacket. Your pilot's coat, it mans you, it's you.

Act 2, scene 2

Charles Stanford's room in the College. Benjamin is having a tutorial. It is late in the Michaelmas term, and Stanford, who has done with the difficulties of a new intake of students, has relaxed his 'spikey authoritarian' mode and is beginning to offer a warmer side to his students, especially, perhaps, to those he believes have substantial talent. 'The list of pupils who (may) grow to a genuine individuality under his tuition' is 'staggering', – to adapt one musicologist. At any rate, Stanford is as generous to talent as he is severe on the inauthentic. His working room is tall and square, like the tower of a cathedral, and the light – sharp resinous light of December – strikes through high windows. There is the cheer of a coal fire; and a piano equips the room; a desk and chairs. Benjamin, who has monitored the mood of Stanford the whole term, now judges that this is the correct moment to broach the subject of the Christmas Carnival. Benjamin is long but steely. He is talented but not attractive. Forbidding, something cold seems to char in him. Stanford pauses in his tuition to answer Benjamin's request.

STANFORD   Yes, I think I can, I think I will come;
the festival is sound, and if well-planned brings
pleasure to music.

BENJAMIN   The students will be pleased, and I am.
And if, sir, you will devise something

STANFORD   Me, or
the student in me?

BENJAMIN   We are students, sir; and though
each needs to hug his talent to himself,
even from a friend's eyes

STANFORD   especially
such a one

BENJAMIN   some contribution
serious and musical

STANFORD   such as the line of women,
their thighs well-regulated to the Chorus.

BENJAMIN   Your order and tact touch what in us are
hidden things.

(Stanford is about to reply when there is a knock.)   Pause.

STANFORD	Enter, please.

(Joseph enters. His hair is tousled. He wears his Severn Pilot's coat, and has tied a pink kerchief about his throat. He carries manuscripts and approaches Stanford diffidently. Nods to Benjamin.)

STANFORD	I am pleased to see you, Gurney. Yes, sit here. This is a good moment for your work.
JOSEPH	Yes?
STANFORD	I purposely brought in your friend who, you know, I value.
JOSEPH	As I do, sir.
STANFORD	Yes, that is your opinion. My reasons are his music is legible

(during this reply to him, Joseph is seen to shift restlessly and to look away from both Stanford and Benjamin.)

> it can be followed,
> however quiet and modest the phrasing, however slight
> the spirt, yet the faint rustle of water
> can be heard. I hear it, it speaks.

JOSEPH	I agree.

(Stanford invites Benjamin to play. Benjamin gets up and, quietly, goes to the piano and plays a few phrases of his own work. It is meant to deprecate himself, but it does not do this. He smirks at Joseph.)

JOSEPH	Yes, sir, I think that, too. And I think that I, too –
STANFORD	you are very sure of yourself.

pause

JOSEPH	Sir allow me to sing – although my voice isn't a great deal. Not being much, the words bring out the music
STANFORD	Fine, then. You touch me; and I hope the music, which has fingers, is better still.

(Benjamin bows to Joseph behind Stanford's back, but by the time Stanford has sensed the performance, and has turned round, Benjamin is composed.)

STANFORD   You are here to write music, and not
shapely rhetoric, not even the pointed
rasp of verse.

JOSEPH   How's that, sir? yes,
my work is untidy,
it is sometimes chaos. But for God's sake,
do not say you can't follow it,
the water does run, as you say sir, it does;
and when I bring another's words to my hands
the music that they have together – is music.
Sir, I've written five songs, please hear one.

(Joseph goes to the piano in the corner of the room, and takes silence for assent. Seats himself, arranges his music, and produces one of his earliest accomplished songs, 'Sleep', – music with the words of Fletcher.)

JOSEPH   *Sleep*

It's Fletcher's words. His music, too,
if I'm honest.

(Fletcher's 'Sleep')

(During the playing of it, Benjamin has stiffened and shows discomposure. Salieri's condition.)

STANFORD   Fine. The spray, the inspiration if you wish,
is controlled. Not an inspired fluke.
Control working imagination. I loved that.

JOSEPH   Sir, I am glad.

STANFORD   *(to Benjamin)*
                Don't you think so?

JOSEPH   Sir, please. Don't push him.

STANFORD   I ask
because I value his judgment; you need not
indulge your embarrassment. Art is
altogether different.

BENJAMIN   This is Joseph, sir,
with a coat of many colours.

STANFORD	*(to Joseph)*
	The fine tact
	of embarrassment, like Keats had. Yet you,
	your person, we don't need
JOSEPH	yes, sir.
STANFORD	*(to Benjamin)*
	And it's because I value
	you as practitioner, as a writer of music
	who practices as if performance were key,
	as if inspiration came a modest second, that I ask.
BENJAMIN	I could do without tact, sir;
	I am a musician. I see that Joseph's work
	is well-done.
STANFORD	More than that, even,
	perhaps?
BENJAMIN	As a writer of what is strong
	I value in you what I believe is in me.
	If my work means anything it is delicate.
	From my own
	I see Joseph's is well-done. I use
	your kind of approval.
STANFORD	His music defies mine.
BENJAMIN	*(very quietly)*
	Then why ask me
STANFORD	I beg you to excuse me. You
	are fine in your own right.
JOSEPH	Before we finish, sir,
	you had a manuscript of mine
STANFORD	*(sifts through a neat stack of papers)*
	You shall have it back. Yes...
	it is not right, though, and... I think I may put
	it this way...and this.
	(corrects with pencil)
	There, my friend,
	that puts it right.

JOSEPH   *(takes it and examines the corrections)*
                                    Well, Sir Charles,
                  I see you've jigged the whole thing. Now
                  I must sail upside-down.

STANFORD   Impudent of you.
                  Go on. Remove yourself.

JOSEPH   *(in anger his Gloucester voice becomes more pronounced)*
                                    I hope you'll give
                  me the chance to knock about something
                  of yours sometime.

                  (Joseph exits)

STANFORD   Yes, remove yourself.
                  The child! Will the war do something to us
                  to change everything? Will it destroy
                  suns and fruits? even in his Gloucestershire –

                  (Benjamin stares at Stanford)

                  as if the apple swirled with yellow were a disease,
                  nothing gives its health again.   *(pause)*   Do you
                  feel sane? The cracks in the plaster
                  are those in the stonework itself.

                  (to Benjamin)

                  In you, the delicacies flow even and deep   *(pause)*
                  Oh, minds are still the same, his narrative's
                  a grimy tumble of bricks. The shed holds
                  the prophet who must have his space, intensity in space,
                  no matter what this war calls out, – and destroys. Genius needs
                  the accumulation of fanged wit
                  in a slant hovel. But why, always,
                  in a shambles, in space fit
                  for the slaughter only of a pig? A kosher act
                  needs hygiene. Couth and wiped.
                  It foams, is bloody. I can take that.
                  But such folding of the brain is a tussle
                  of farmyard father and son. Must it be?
                  Or is the mark of mere genius, disorder? Are these
                  our times, the small
                  pretentious mudded hut, smirched,
                  wassail spilled over its pikes of wood?

44

the brain is no fortress, but kind, genial,
a community of nuzzling forms, upright, domestic –
Benjamin, I would weep, if it weren't
mirth mingled with these blotched shapes which he forms.
There is the talent
England needs to make live what lies inert,
like a dried moth –
the small antlered hall, where walking-stick
and barometer subdue the mind to custom.
A land needs soft accomplishment,
the shoot's modesty. Track the mind
and you may see perfect intelligence,
when we assist people, fine, well-tuned students.
And your mind, and his, grow deeper, sensitive
by more than each self. He is my work. Please, help me,
assist this ragged form,
if it pleases you, so it may size up
itself, and find commodity.

BENJAMIN   Yes, sir, after my own work.

(Exit Benjamin)

STANFORD   Yes, of course. But your house is a fine
being, not threatened with madness.

Act 2, scene 3

Joseph is in his room in Fulham. In digs. It is a long room, not unlike what he had in his Barton Street house. He has moved from the urban petit-bourgeois of Gloucester to the urban working-class village of a part of London; south-west London, north of the Thames.

The room is ordinary enough, but the rectangle seems a bit narrower at one end, as if it had lost a part of its perspective. Two doors. One, right back, which leads to a small bathroom; the other, front left. Joseph lolls on one side of the bed; Benjamin sits in one of the two upright chairs, and wears his glasses.

BENJAMIN   Why so erratic?   *pause*
             Not a thing at breakfast.   *pause*   True, isn't it? and then
             at midday a rush of buns, later,
             cream, jam, and scones – why?

JOSEPH   Do I?

BENJAMIN   Why do you say 'do I', over and over?

JOSEPH	Who does?
BENJAMIN	Your stomach must be in poor shape. *pause*
JOSEPH	When we lived in Barton Street
BENJAMIN	yes?
JOSEPH	My father brought strawberries, also the green frilly leafs of spinach. I loved that. Fresh peas; colours with smells, like a lock opening its fresh water.
BENJAMIN	A lock doesn't open water.
JOSEPH	What doesn't? *pause* – a weir, pouring marble. Then there was steam barges, stinking of sulphur and something like tar. There was a chain
BENJAMIN	a rachet. They had them in Bristol.
JOSEPH	Were you born there?
BENJAMIN	Not, at least, in your culture.
JOSEPH	It feels to me that, not including Gloucester, your culture and mine, is like. Very alike. When you pull open the pod, just two peas, squashed together, with flat sides.
BENJAMIN	You've got to do something with yourself.
JOSEPH	Who?
BENJAMIN	Those five songs were very fine. Now do something else.
JOSEPH	*(getting off the bed)* Thank you.
BENJAMIN	You getting up?
JOSEPH	No.
BENJAMIN	Offended?
JOSEPH	I said nothing about that.

46

BENJAMIN	Or joining

BENJAMIN   Or joining
the Army? *(mimicking)* It's a great life;
see all over the male body; it's free. It makes
men of men, of the lad
a cruel boy.

JOSEPH   *I* don't want to join. Neither to be shot
nor gassed. I'm sane aren't I?

BENJAMIN   *(looks at him curiously)*
                                     Maybe.

JOSEPH   Aren't I? well, leave it where it is.   *pause*
I had a letter from Miss Betty today: my first
woman-friend. She encouraged me,
all along.

BENJAMIN   A prodigy.

JOSEPH   No, she wasn't.
She helped me live with my talent. I felt, then,
as if there was another person
in this body lent to me, who wasn't friendly;
the whole time he was at me: do it,
he said, you must do it.

BENJAMIN   What?

JOSEPH   so instead
of feeling insane – for the music that came
– write it, Betty said. It will be,
so let it be.

BENJAMIN   How
will you do it in the Army?

JOSEPH   How – are you handing out...
white feathers?

BENJAMIN   Read
me the letter.

JOSEPH   *(reads)*

But I've changed my mind about your never enlisting. This is a war to
end war. The only feathers I have I keep in my eiderdown. But do you
not think, my dear friend, that you ought at least to give the medical
board another try? For if they gave you a proper inspection, and then
it's no good, -- I would never suggest it again. But you are a fit man,

	with a strong constitution. If you put aside your indigestion, you're just as strong as can be. Stronger than Benjamin even. He can't; you, at least, might try again.
BENJAMIN	Syrup.
JOSEPH	It may be. What she says worries me, though.
BENJAMIN	Are you ready to join?
JOSEPH	Maybe. No, I'll never enlist. Never.
BENJAMIN	(imitates a marching soldier with a rifle, left arm extended at right angles to his body. He believes he is being comical. His long, lanky flesh is also comical, as if he and it would never fit the Army. But there is also a strange cold fieriness in his actions)
	Women of England say, Go. (pause) So do I.
JOSEPH	Do you? do you, in fact?
BENJAMIN	No. That is to say, yes.
JOSEPH	Do you really say that? Must I fight? Oh, must I be a cat, claws extended, and get killed, and become muck? Is that it? Because you're not fit, for because your eyes are slovenly, must I? Your eyes, working which way, every way, wanting focus, though not attention. Must I, therefore?
BENJAMIN	So, don't do it.
JOSEPH	Maybe I should offer myself. Again. Must I? – nothing can justify war.
BENJAMIN	Then don't.
JOSEPH	Besides, why should I die for her? Or for my mother? She's had her half-life.
BENJAMIN	Then don't.
JOSEPH	(Looks at Benjamin. No response.) Too many destroyed in this stupid business. Sorley, Brzeska – the sculptor –

BENJAMIN	*(quickly)* and we say nothing, besides, of all those without a name, without talent
JOSEPH	I didn't say they weren't valuable
BENJAMIN	no name. No damned name whatsoever
JOSEPH	I didn't say that. I didn't mean that. I just don't hear them – because – they nave no name.
BENJAMIN	That's right. Muck, as you say. *pause* Have you written to her?
JOSEPH	Who?
BENJAMIN	Have you written her a letter?
JOSEPH	Yes
BENJAMIN	Is it private? Never mind.
JOSEPH	*(reads loudly and aggressively)*

you are not, except in an imaginary sense, called on to lay down *your* life. Why then do you feel justified in encouraging other *men* to do so? Oughtn't you, in fairness, to be trying to stop death?

BENJAMIN	If you don't fight, how will these values, all these precious commodities, these oils, the oil in the stone of olive, how will these get preserved? *(pause)* How? the charred stones on a Gloucester beach? The eggs in a nest clustered like testicles.
JOSEPH	Is the Germans out to destroy –
BENJAMIN	for they will come we know

(Joseph is silent)

       – travel the downs, the bare wind is military now, it speaks fear of invasion. The chips of flint look like bones.

JOSEPH	I can't stop it.
BENJAMIN	Thousands might

JOSEPH	those thousands have died already. No, I will not. *pause*
	If I were an insect, the small bird
	would be a large one. This War
	of irreconcileable feelings, the passions struck
	together, of kind old maids and the younger ones
	armed with feathers....

pause

I'm going for a piss.

(exits right)

Benjamin, alone, becomes restless. He moves round the room inspecting its contents. On the bed over which the covers have been twitched, as if to hide soiled sheets, is a teapot. He picks it up, and, judging by the weight, finds it partly full. He exclaims, and puts it down. There is dust on the dressing table mirror. He writes something in it, stares at what he has written – then abruptly erases it. He moves back to the bed and his foot jars against a chamber-pot. He exclaims again; catching sight of some music manuscript Joseph is working, he picks it up

BENJAMIN	To be able to do this! you don't deserve yourself, Joseph,
	I could envy a man
	for less than this.

(There is a knock at the door front left.)

So soon

The door opens. Elizabeth enters. She looks pretty – but it is as if what she would now be prepared to take would be consolation, not happiness. As if she were incapable now of seizing, or gently taking, happiness were it offered her. Her face suggests luck – that is, the quality of receptivity which attracts good fortune; but the strength required to retain and use it is missing. She comes towards Benjamin, her hand outstretched

ELIZABETH	Joseph is...?
BENJAMIN	*(calling)*
	Joseph.
ELIZABETH	Don't bother.
	(enter Joseph)
JOSEPH	Yes?
	(sees Elizabeth, and goes to her.)
	It's lovely to see you. *pause*
ELIZABETH	*(smiling, but serious)*
	Are you ready for poor news?
	(to Benjamin) excuse me.

JOSEPH	News is always poor, Eliza.
ELIZABETH	Is it all right – I mean if your friend
	(Joseph nods)
	The College has your scholarship at its discretion.
JOSEPH	I know.
ELIZABETH	Its discretion is bureaucratic, like the Church –
JOSEPH	What does that mean?
ELIZABETH	– its spiritual power's subservient to the State like the spire of St George's –
JOSEPH	Eliza!
ELIZABETH	the figure isn't Christ; it's George the First, at the top.
JOSEPH	Am I to laugh? *pause* So what is it, Eliza?
	(Benjamin is prowling around the room)
	(to Benjamin)
	Will you stop, please.
BENJAMIN	*(stops)* Shall I go?
ELIZABETH	the College Scholarship is discretionary. Joseph, not with me, – not angry with me, please. It is terrible to say it. First you must have a medical, and, if you're fit, enlist.
JOSEPH	And if I don't?
ELIZABETH	The money vanishes, like dew.
JOSEPH	What happens if I'm fit and join?
ELIZABETH	Then the money remains. The College shines, like a bead of dew.

JOSEPH   I'll go. Everyone wants my body—
              for the army. If
              they'll have me, I'll go, for my medical.
              Have old men inspect my testicles, handle them,
              have me bend over, and my anus amuse them,
              the bony muscle sticking out of my thigh's back,
              like a jib. If they tolerate
              my frail digestion, I'll go.

BENJAMIN   You will have to.

              *(Elizabeth makes despairing gestures with her arms, opening them
              towards Joseph as if with compassion)*

              I'll go now.

JOSEPH   All right then.

              (A glance held between Joseph and Benjamin, then exit Benjamin)

*Joseph and Elizabeth stand before each other; quite close, with a distance between
them they both recognize. Beneath her shyness is timidity. Under her reserve, more
reserve. They are drawn to each other but cannot find the means to complete the
relationship yet. They are glad to be with each other, but there is pain in their contact.*

*Elizabeth turns from Joseph and starts to wander about his room. She does this in such
a way as to emphasize not the size of the room but the amount of space in it. Space is
ambiguous; it can suggest freedom, or loneliness. During the beginning of this section
she should be making deft, quite meaningful changes to the feel of Joseph's room. She
does this by the clever re-arrangement of some of the objects in it – a few of which are
personal. All the objects are to be placed in such a way that their re-arrangement is
noticeable, affecting the surface of Joseph's life.*

JOSEPH   First, I think of enlisting, and trying to get my head
              blown off. Then, of getting some manual job –
              anything but let this dyspeptic serpent crawl
              about me; but it seems I'm not fit for anything. I know
              I've written five songs.   *pause*
              You would forgive me if you knew how wretched
              I feel.

ELIZABETH   Do you mind
              if I change this; it lets more light through?

              (moves an object)

JOSEPH   Do so, please. Then, again, I think of
              enlisting if they'll have me. Though it's against

52

	all my principles of justice,
	though I'd be doing the most criminal thing
	a man could.
ELIZABETH	Thousands are.
JOSEPH	More

than that. Then I say,
to my dogged part – I have a fear my frame seems spindly,
as if at my medical exam, my parts would wag,
as I ran about for the doctors.
I fear to seem ridiculous.

ELIZABETH *(comes up and puts her arms round his neck)*

So do
we all fear.

JOSEPH   Perhaps I am.

ELIZABETH *(releases him with a sigh)* No.

JOSEPH   I wanted to join the medical corps – the idea
of killing upsets me. But I want to write music.
That's what I'm fit for, I think.
Tell me, how does a man write music
and carry a stretcher? When I listen, it rises in me,
I hear it scrape across my mind, which is
my self's echo.

pause

I love Gloucestershire,
I'd fight for it. If I have to go, I will go

pause

Do you love me?

ELIZABETH   What chance have I,
if you get killed?

JOSEPH   and my scholarship stops

ELIZABETH   nothing is what you'll get.

JOSEPH   For some women,
love would still be something.

ELIZABETH   I didn't say
I loved you.   *(strong pause)*   And if you got killed
where would I be?

JOSEPH	Thousands of good men
ELIZABETH	thousands

of good women have misery enough
to press them into the earth.
I wish I could have just sex.

JOSEPH	Have you?
ELIZABETH	Not just sex.
BENJAMIN	But for my sickness

I'd have been a great child.   *(pause)*   Have you noticed
how the morals bleat out loud. It's all all right.
Some men go; their families can afford it
if their sons are destroyed, their husbands, there's no matter.
Money lives. Bright as the sun, more
suffusing. The poorer ones, me,
the ones dyspeptic with poverty, we escape: we
are glad. If we're buried in mud, or chalk, our bones
indistinguishable from that, why
there's a relief, because we hate it here.

ELIZABETH	You ought not to, love.
JOSEPH	Never before

have I heard you say that.

ELIZABETH	If you're going to die,

I'm going to say it.

JOSEPH	Do you want me?
ELIZABETH	I want me, I am

first. And if I do want you, it's after
I have me. Do you understand?

JOSEPH	It feels hard, but I understand

– I feel like a kind of whore.

ELIZABETH	why?
JOSEPH	Yes,

I do.

ELIZABETH	Joseph, please, take me to some place,

take me for tea somewhere. Let me pay. Take me
out, where there is a waitress, and the woman

wears a small frill above her breasts, Joseph, please,
take me....

pause

if the rooms are quiet, without music;
the rustle of dried bees. Just that.

(She takes him by the hand. They exit)

Act 2, scene 4

(In Joseph's digs. He is on his bed asleep.)

JOSEPH   How to make a jib that lifts the maiden fern.
If a spray of leaf,
tooth, or hair, abandons itself
to the claws that should be hands, –
intent on handling – it will crush.
The leaves crush foolishly and spray in handling.

How take nature in modern hands, how give
the dockland man, his hefty male child
and cheeky painted daughter, the bent contour of earth, –
a pink campion
stepping on black soil. The barge

sifts through pasture, its working man
smudges his fag in oil and clay, this tandem
of dirt.

*Enter Stanford and Florence Gurney, mummer-like, a bit coarse in their movements
and a little stiff, as though part of Joseph's dreaming. Theirs, and every other person's
speech in the scene should be slightly different from their natural waking talk.*

FLORENCE   Hard work is verse; hardest of it all.
Causes fits.

(Enter Benjamin awkwardly.)

BENJAMIN   Pardon me.

(Enter Sloeman, and Betty with a bayonet.)

BETTY   The Army. Into it. For a stiff dose of pencil. That's what you require.

And gas-coloured feathers.

FLORENCE   Not the Army.

BENJAMIN   *(sheepishly)*

Where, then? In all this world, I should like to know

55

STANFORD	to the Music Reformatory. Get rid of the verse.
JOSEPH	But verse is inspiration. I could write it even in the Army.
BENJAMIN	Yes, sir. The New Year says it; the Army whirls its brain, its smashed recumbent strands
STANFORD	*(with excitement and sudden clarity)* to the Music Deformatory! *(with sudden realization)* But suffer no direct heat.
BENJAMIN	*(comes towards Joseph, grinning)* We need a violent solution.
JOSEPH	To what?
BETTY	To what! To violence.

pause

ELIZABETH	Love, we are not joking.
JOSEPH	I know that.
BETTY	*(raising the large bayonet)* This is it; we must have death for our going-on with – precious sacrifice, to perpetrate more life.
FLORENCE	I will not have my son killed in his soul's presence.
BETTY	Who said he had been chosen for sacrifice? he should be that fortunate.

pause

But, but, Mother Gurney, that willing sacrifice must ensure our continuity. By these paws...*(shows what should be hands; they are animal claws)*

pause

The War! The War!

SLOEMAN	*(in continuation)* The prism of selflessness.

BETTY   *(at attention, as if imitating a male soldier, but with a long skirt on)*
                (shouts)
                Yes, sir.

They all crowd round Joseph, and kneel to him praying forgiveness; and, at the same time, rejoice in his existence, since death is to ensure their life as a group. Only Florence Gurney does not join in, and stands apart, covering her face with her hands. The word each speaks, one after the other, sometimes together though, sometimes out of synchronization, is 'forgiveness'. It rises to a moderated climax. They scatter about him, and one – it is Benjamin – comes with his blade, to plunge it into Joseph's body. As he comes to perform this, his face is transfigured with joy and relief. At one moment it is as though he grinned. Then the grin vanishes, and the face resumes its expression of joy.

BENJAMIN   *(to Joseph)*
                You!

                (he raises the long blade which can clearly be seen to be a bayonet)

                This is my best office. As I strike you, look at me
                for I spill your life. Sweeten this earth
                I stand on, and in the clean wheat, rest,
                for the flat toy of our health, or remedy – death.
                I hear the lock-gates opening. Now –

                (He plunges the bayonet into Joseph's body, smiling, and, as he does so, Joseph screams and breaks away. Figures dissolve.)

JOSEPH   I was flat and crushed in sleep. Now I am waking
                from myself. Rather the War
                than this. Rather the bleak trench
                than this hunger I famish on; these pleached tangled
                boughs, than a slashed hedge. I make no sense
                of any life I was in. The lock-keeper opens
                his gate, that's what I know. And the water flows
                through, level with the plain.

Act 3, scene 1*

Empty stage. Elizabeth's College office. A knock. A pause. Benjamin enters, and seeing no-one there starts to look at papers on Elizabeth's desk. He discovers a letter – Joseph's to Elizabeth, and starts to read it.

BENJAMIN   But lord, humanity is strange. Our Corporal, who keeps a betting pool in people's survival – no, God damn it, not survival, but death – like a man who holds you by your collar, up against a stone wall, and punches you until your head splits – oh, excuse melodrama – this Corporal makes a profit thereby.

Act 3, scene 2

'The Book'

English trench. Ironmask, a huge man of the West Riding. Gurney; Handshone, a Jew – each, like Ironmask, Privates. Corporal Snatcher keeps the 'book', his drudge, Private Fly. Other solder. Evening, early summer. Corporal is going round the platoon collecting money, with the aid of Fly, and is marking off each payment in The Book.

HANDSHONE   *(playing with revolver Russian roulette style)*

There's your dice. And each time
we go over...I don't know *(slowly points gun at his own head)*
nor do you *(slowly turns gun on Corporal)*

(The Corporal is – for the moment – frightened – until Handshone mockingly breaks open the revolver to reveal its chambers are empty)

CORPORAL   I could charge yer.

IRONMASK   Tha' could, tha's tried; nither one
profited.

CORPORAL   Yer's warned. *(to Handshone)* The Book is common
practice. *(to Ironmask)* Pay, or close yer mouth.

IRONMASK   Ah'll pay, an tha' knows.

CORPORAL   Yes.

FLY   You are right, corporal.

---

*Omit this scene if the theme of the next – The Book – emerges clearly in the playing.

IRONMASK   Fly, tha' as
                coloured wings, wha's gloss is flattery.

HANDSHONE I'm leavin' your Book, Corporal.

CORPORAL   And then there's
                the money loaned

IRONMASK   tha's t'hole
                rejiment as borrowed fro' thee wi tha meddlesome
                notes
CORPORAL   nothin' in King's Regulations
                ter say yer can't.

HANDSHONE   You worked it out,
                Corporal.

CORPORAL   'an many as wants ter loan
                from me.

IRONMASK   'Appen thar is.

CORPORAL   'an on the nail gits it

HANDSHONE and they give something back
                more than they received.

CORPORAL   Private, yer
                full av shite.

JOSEPH   Am I in the Book?

                (everyone laughs)

                what is it? why am I laughed at?

                                    pause

                I am laughed at

IRONMASK   It's t'silent pandemonium
                of innocence ter not reco'nize
                'is spanglin' greed – tha's learned some.
                Tha' uses
                that tha' knows.   *(pause)*   Corporal's nor richer fer it.

CORPORAL   Yer on a charge.

IRONMASK   Am I?
                Thee and who else?

FLY   Corporal, you're in
                the right.

IRONMASK   Fly, if tha lived
                    by tha naime, tha'd drop off t'ceiling;
                    every part of tha suction's gone. *(to Joseph)* The Corporal's
                    a sort o' Jew.

JOSEPH   He loans his money
                    out?

HANDSHONE   Not right, Ironmask.
                    I'm a Jew: my loanin' returns
                    without interest.

IRONMASK   Tha's raaght.
                    Tha' gi's, tha' gits back
                    an' tha charges nowt.

CORPORAL   Leave it.

                    (Fly starts to collect money)

JOSEPH   Why
                    should I give him money?

IRONMASK   For if tha's done
                    Corporal visits tha' mither. No, 'E doan't though.
                    But if tha gits the bullet, we split yer stake
                    an' if we gits it, t'wager is yer's

JOSEPH   the Corporal takes a slice, each time

HANDSHONE   every
                    time.

FLY   And he's a lot of book-work.

IRONMASK   Tha's gobby a bit o' 'is phlegm.

HANDSHONE   What if, Corporal,
                    you got no percent against us killed?

CORPORAL   Leave it...

HANDSHONE   then what if, Corporal,
                    you made a Book, but no deaths,
                    no divvy up?

CORPORAL   Leave it!

HANDSHONE Beg to report, Corporal –

CORPORAL   Leave it, I said,   *(pause)*   The Book gaas
                    up ter two-an-six next month.

60

FLY	Shite!
HANDSHONE	What malice, Corporal, makes yer do it? death's not so expensive.
CORPORAL	Drop dead.

(Joseph gives money. Corporal and Fly have now finished collecting. Corporal exits. Ironmask makes a gesture of aiming a rifle at Fly. Exit fly strutting, but a bit crestfallen.)

IRONMASK	Tha's a fly, too, tha' summer days fragile nor tin. *(to Joseph)* Doan' gi anything. If tha' takes nowt, tha' returns nowt. Tha'll be raaght then. Mind, if tha' needs fer beer, then oot it comes. But due-day, e's sharp as a tat.

(Cries heard from a distance. Corporal runs in. Shouts.)

CORPORAL	Stand-to. Man the fire-steps. Gurney get movin'.

(machine-gun fire. Stops)

CORPORAL	They're comin naw — steady fire, commence

(Each one fires through loops in trenches; then the Germans leap into the trenches, and hand-to-hand fighting ensues — always the most terrible part of combat. Handshone is getting the worst of his encounter; Joseph goes to help him, but Handshone is bayonetted.)

JOSEPH	*(holds Handshone in his arms)* What is it?
HANDSHONE	I've my cards.

dies

JOSEPH	Wait, I'll write my music; it will say, it's murder.

(Joseph relinquishes Handshone and starts to kill the remaining Germans. There is something, not desperate, but inspired, in his fighting. He fights like an angel, a fallen one. The attack is now beaten off; Joseph continues to stab, and stab again, a German whom he has killed, and who is clearly dead)

Perhaps I kill for Gloucestershire. Yes,
I do. The blither of them churchbells. Yes.
An' for the Corporal's usury, I do.

Stab stab. I'll do it. I work
for Gloucestershire. Its slurry trickles
the occasional flower, wet and thick.

Put it upon the Jew.

(Ironmask comes to him and puts a restraining hand)

IRONMASK   He's laike shoddy, laike wool.
'E's terrestrial, laid thar; an tha' sees —
tha' may see it fer thysel' that 'e is.   *(pause)*   Fight
wi' cunnin', skill — but mercy. Tha's shewed, today,
a nikkid patch o' thasel'. The man
was brave, strong; but it's as if
tha' tak 'im in tha' arms,
tha' groond 'im against tha' — 'is boones brak,
'is blood burst.

*(Ironmask begins to lead Joseph off. Scraps of paper meet them,
blowing along the trench. Ironmask stoops, on his haunches reads
one.)*

JOSEPH   What?

*(Ironmask does not reply, but tears it up. Then he reads another, and
tears it up. He begins to laugh. A mix of triumph and disbelief. Gruff,
as if it were difficult to laugh on account of the aggression. This
agitates Joseph.)*

JOSEPH   Tell me.

(Joseph starts to laugh, but soon stops.)

IRONMASK   It's the 'hole rejiment's money —
I mean t'Corporal's...

                    Looks up grinning.

'E that were lost, is foond.

JOSEPH   What?

IRONMASK   Cans't tha not read, 'ere
                         hands him one
                         mind
tha' tears it oop, when tha' 'as.

JOSEPH   What?

(Ironmask starts to tear up all the I.O.U.s he can gather up)

IRONMASK   T'wind
shakes 'er fithers, an 'is substance blews;
t' promissory scraps – ower cash –
'is power – 'is notes of ower abliteration;
tha' sees, a soft wind blaws 'is money awaa'.

Act 3, scene 3

Late June 1917. Elizabeth's office in the College. Desk, piano. Dark room. Benjamin is waiting for her. Standing still near door left. Goes to her desk, right, and finds a letter.

BENJAMIN   It seems I must again bear it.

reads letter aloud

"This Corporal keeps a betting pool in people's survival, and makes a profit thereby. A month or two previous he lost some IOUs, and now seems fair set to get us gassed. He will have us practice with the cylinders, and we must mind him as much as we must the direction of the wind...Thankyou for all your letters. They keep alive in me a resolution not to be broken by the Army, as some men are broken; keep alive hope, and memory of the pleasure that filled me in your music room....The trenches aren't the place for music; guns fix patches of white noise onto the mind – Yet I have produced four songs; not much creation for a year but I am grateful for – I mean, I am pleased. One came to birth in a disused Trench Mortar Emplacement."

Gesture of exasperation; crushes letter in his hand

In that you breathe, Gurney;
restore the mind to its jealous fame.

He replaces crushed letter, then picks it up again. Smooths it out, stands with it, no movement in his face, as if his being had come to a stop. A noise, then the door opens slowly, and Elizabeth enters her room with Stanford. He looks tired, as if fewer students had upon his energy an effect inverse to the expected one.

ELIZABETH   I have some news.

STANFORD   Good?

ELIZABETH   all of it
                  disturbs. I'll read it you
                  – I mean Joseph's music concerns you

BENJAMIN   *(discovered)*

                  all of us.

ELIZABETH   *(taking letter from Benjamin)*
                          Joseph writes that –
                  (reads) "guns fix patches of white noise onto the mind – Yet I have
                  produced four songs. The people I am with" *(stops and looks oddly
                  at Benjamin)* "The people I am with, who are part of me, are an
                  influence to fulfil my music with humanity."
                  He means it. I feel; that's not guff
                  though it may sound so.

                          (to Benjamin) You look displeased.

BENJAMIN   No, no.

ELIZABETH   Oh, what's the use?

STANFORD   Dear Elizabeth, Gurney's well –

ELIZABETH   he speaks of
                  his four songs.
                  His brightness, white with fear.

STANFORD   Four songs;
                  such abundance among the rooted stones
                  it overflows them. I have them too

ELIZABETH   And we can hear them? No, wait: Joseph says

                  "Our Corporal seems fair set to get us gassed. He will have us
                  practice with the cylinders, and we must mind him as much as we
                  must the direction of the wind. But I keep alive in me the resolution
                  not to be broken by the Army, as some men are."
                                          under
                  the jocular voice rigged to suit friends,
                  his fear, that I'm afraid for.

STANFORD   You should not,
                  Elizabeth, have read out
                  his letter

BENJAMIN   why?

STANFORD	*(to Elizabeth)*
	It excites,
	the excitation is a rhetoric of fear; in you
	Gurney's voice exaggerates, and speaks
	your fears.
BENJAMIN	I see. That is plausible.
STANFORD	*(to Benjamin)*
	With due respect,
	it's Elizabeth I'm concerned for. *(to Elizabeth)* Gentle
	woman such as you. You should
	be let to rest, poised like dew,
	and in that poise, have
	his letter's substance, not your voice,
	work in you.
BENJAMIN	*(looking at Stanford)*
	Forgive me, sir,
	I'd no intention to intrude.
ELIZABETH	*(to Benjamin)* But you think
BENJAMIN	It's the gas, the cylinders, the Corporal.
STANFORD	*(ironic)*
	Benjamin, is there something about the army
	you don't know?
BENJAMIN	Sir, there must be.
ELIZABETH	But if the Corporal is uncaring
BENJAMIN	if the Corporal
	commits a misdemeanour – is that
	the correct term – or if he's trying
	to fix something
STANFORD	*(fearful)*
	that is not implied
	in the letter
BENJAMIN	shouldn't Gurney report him?
ELIZABETH	that's right
	isn't it?

STANFORD	How report
	your superior, he a notch above you
	in close and constant authority,
	to the superior remote above him?
	It might do Gurney great harm.

pause

BENJAMIN	I feel
	it might.

STANFORD	Elizabeth, I have asked a student to come
	and sing one of Gurney's songs. A fine one – all are fine,
	so fine we must hear one.

BENJAMIN	Now?

STANFORD	But now, of course. Why not "now"?

BENJAMIN	Sir,
	can the song have been practised, are
	students to do it justice

STANFORD	each of us is student. The water flows
	and stones do not block it

BENJAMIN	But what if
	clumsy fire consume?
	What if it make dust of stone

STANFORD	we do
	not have students like that: War
	or no War. We have standards,
	we have students; the two meet

pause

	and what can you mean,
	fire and stone?

BENJAMIN	it doesn't matter; it does, though.
	It could spoil Gurney's makings

STANFORD	what I have read will not spoil.

Student appears in doorway

(to student)

Here she is.

Please, be seated.

Enter young woman, a student. She is shy, but firm; as if the reserve came from a sense of what she might do rather than what she could not.

MARY   I have the song here.
                 Shall I, sir?

ELIZABETH   Yes we want
                 to hear one.

MARY   One, is all
                 I can do now. It's Gurney's poem, 'Severn Meadows'.

She goes over to piano

                 (to Elizabeth)

                 Will you play?

Elizabeth goes over to piano, sits and plays. They perform Gurney's 'Severn Meadows'.

                              Silence

BENJAMIN   Queer talent, of erotic elegy.

                 Dismemberment in mud, on wire;
                 the strange flocculence of ash, its virtues for scouring,
                 as the Burgundy women know;
                 elegy in gentleness deploring violence. I celebrate
                 Gurney's talent, the undeserving body in which
                 the dyspeptic serpent twines,
                 dissevering ease from talent, fulfilment
                 from creation – the great crawler
                 exacting penalty from whatever's good to Gurney

                 Strange talent, of erotic elegy.

STANFORD   Yes, the man and the work; but he makes the work.
                 It causes in me a breadth of moisture – in the eye
                 and in the tight chest's midst. I love it.
                 The man, your friend, his enharmonic
                 talent, sliding about,
                 but with all energies, wry, passionate
                 and aware – what is there to say of him.
                 He is a man, not lovable, but needy
                 of care.

BENJAMIN   He hardly knows his talent's value.

STANFORD	The more

his innocence then, to give that talent,
the eye and its slithering beam, its due

ELIZABETH   *(pulling back)*

but we always
must be critical of who we care for
whose work we love.

STANFORD   *(exasperated)*   Yes Elizabeth,
yes, if you must.

                                   pause

After the war

BENJAMIN   after it

STANFORD   when it's done
and has ground half its young men to meal,
and half of them's remaining, Gurney
will have back his scholarship. Meanwhile
the army holds together a split man –
binding him
authoritatively

BENJAMIN   he'll come back,
if the army preserve him.

ELIZABETH   Please don't
name that pain

BENJAMIN   I am sorry. I meant
no distress, only personal bitterness.

STANFORD   Benjamin, you must do your music;
the war has spared you – health and eyesight,
in their true defect, – to use your talent,
so that you make your

BENJAMIN   I hate my talent,
against all others.   *(pause)*   I do. I preserve
the fake enzyme digesting its own body
where there's no food.   *(pause)*   No, I offer
contrast, where it should be comparison. –
Other's talent, compared with mine. Excuse me.

STANFORD   Not being in the army strains you.

BENJAMIN	The army
	is no man's. A compulsion
	of ghosts.
ELIZABETH	You said we had to fight
BENJAMIN	I wouldn't want to be gassed. I could
	spare my life, not my mutilation,
	my thinning out of self on a wound.
	If there's no God to hear my work,
	despite the scrupulous craftsmanliness –
STANFORD	your's is to survive
ELIZABETH	Yes, be glad,
	friend; as Joseph will be to learn
	how you like his song.
STANFORD	You have
	your talent, Benjamin
BENJAMIN	Competence.

exit Benjamin

Act 3, scene 4

A Trench. Ironmask, Gurney, Fly, Other solider.
They wheel in gas cylinders; the wind is blowing lightly upon their backs.

CORPORAL	The Adjutant
	is ter lecture yer on gas; get fell in.

They do

ADJUTANT	Men, I shan't lecture you. I hope I have
	some helpful things to say. Gas is
	a modern invention, the first weapon
	– on how you're privileged to use it.
IRONMASK	Ah'm sure
JOSEPH	a noble fool
IRONMASK	'an faithful to 'is stripes,
	'is stripes upon ower back.

Corporal glares

ADJUTANT	Other wars, other weapons.

Laughs. The soliders, who are lined up diagonally so that the audience sees face and profile, stiffen slightly.

	Creçy had
gunpowder.	*laughs*

In their Civil War, Americans
fired a machine-gun, still, for some,
over-rated.

FLY 'E thinks soer; *(gestures)* but we may all
be mowed

ADJUTANT But all agree
gas is the best answer. You'll say,
Fritz has gas too. Ours is
lethal, more so, I think. It wastes
the lungs. You will
shortly unleash this.

He scrutinizes them as if he expects to find on their faces an answer to some unasked question

ADJUTANT The Corporal will treat you fairly. If there's any doubt
conditions are adverse
for the discharge of our gas, Corporal will,
"not use gas now", he'll say. Corporal is
expert in this lethal...Men, are there
any questions?

Silence

IRONMASK *(to Joseph)*
How is there such waste
o' breath?

(Exit Adjutant)

CORPORAL Line up be'ind
yer cylinders.

IRONMASK *(to Joseph)*
Tha' must expect
tha' best breath, now, an' be lak
th' honey coomb.

CORPORAL Quiet.

IRONMASK Corporal, tha' thinks to silence us, ah' sees.

JOSEPH	*(to Ironmask)*
	Why do you say so?
CORPORAL	Put yer 'ands on the release 'andle.

They do so

CORPORAL	Now's yer chance to put this across Fritz.
FLY	I 'opes so'er, Corporal.
CORPORAL	'An I 'opes...yer makes this a success. I'm retirin' ter the 'ut *(points to dug-out)* besides yer. I'm partic'lar to observe the effects.
IRONMASK	*(to Joseph)*
	So that's it.
	(to the Corporal)
	In th' 'ut, Corporal?
CORPORAL	*(grinning slightly)*
	I'm watchin' yer, like I said.
FLY	I've been watchin' you-er, too, Corporal.
CORPORAL	Get ready now.
IRONMASK	*(to Joseph)*
	Breathe in.
JOSEPH	What for?
IRONMASK	Do it; put breath in tha'

Joseph breathes in heavily and continues to do so

IRONMASK	yes, as if th' animals that strutted, prowled, an'squirmed, – as if they circulates through tha'. *(pause)* That's al' tha' ivver can 'ave.

CORPORAL   *(shouts from opening of dug-out)*
            Right – set it off.

Puts on mask and watches. The soldiers release the gas which hardly travels towards the German Lines, and instead begins to envelop them. They shut off the cylinders, but there is gas in the air. They begin to cough.

JOSEPH   What have I done?

IRONMASK   Tha's gassed

            (Corporal emerges from dug-out, in mask, and beats gas gong. The soldiers struggle to fit on their masks. It is late for that.)

JOSEPH   my songs moist
            with air from Gloucester

IRONMASK   save it

JOSEPH   noise from the earthen cavern,
            a vacuum
            of music in hills...overlook the scribbled
            town of England.

            (Ironmask can not reply. Coughs and reels.)

                        I am gassed
            inside me...froth bites the lip
            of my breathing

IRONMASK   save it

JOSEPH   I want strength

IRONMASK   in tha' silence

JOSEPH   the animals
            have deserted me

OTHER   our gas
SOLDIER   is strong.

Act 4, scene 1

(A room off the main ward of an Edinburgh hospital. A January afternoon, 1918. Joseph in bed, Benjamin visiting. The room is white.)

BENJAMIN   An odd room, as if memory had
            blanked.

JOSEPH   Seems odd?

BENJAMIN	so white,
	distant a place.
	So alpine and pure.
JOSEPH	Tell me, simply –.
	They paint me here more white than I am.
	I keep hearing
	a voice, pure as pebbly frost,
	the greyish white of semen.
	'Queer' it says, like a flute. And then,
	'chorister Gurney, chorister Gurney', in
	a kind of jeer. I am no man, it seems.
BENJAMIN	*(looking round)*
	The gas though.
	You've had a terrible sickness.
JOSEPH	Yes
BENJAMIN	To choke, as if the air
	we had went bad. The choking, the iodine
	rasp...
JOSEPH	Here's a bit of luck; "owing to slight
	indigestion, presumably due to gas"...wink, wink,
	I'm laid up here, where they'll keep me.
	By the way, some time ago Sassoon walked up to his Colonel,
	No more fighting, he said,
	for me or anyone. Flashes of blue fire. They,
	in a house, solved the man, dissolved him
	in a house – 'here', they said, 'recover your wits
	in this house of nuts.'
BENJAMIN	This is
	a hospital, Gurney.
	(Enter Nurse Jenny Hawthornden. Joseph looks hungrily after her.)
JENNY	Joseph,
	you look well today.
	(looks slyly at him)
	Let me plump up
	the pillow.
	(to Benjamin)
	Who're you?

JOSEPH	A friend, a musician.
JENNY	That's plenty to go on with; go, Joseph, down in your bed. *(looks at him)* Do as I say. *(to Benjamin)* You will not tax him, friend, will you?

hesitates then exits

BENJAMIN	She's brief
JOSEPH	and sharp. *pause* And she's who I love – that's Jenny. The Scottish day is touched by her. She tinges it with hard radiance, a rim, a rind of pure light. That's she. And I love her.
BENJAMIN	I see it. And what of Elizabeth, and your music
JOSEPH	what of... whatever happens to me, a wink, a spasm of gas hiding in indigestion – a burn from a cigarette

(Benjamin offers Joseph a cigarette. Joseph takes it.)

BENJAMIN	Oh, you do smoke now?
JOSEPH	*(shouting)* No.
BENJAMIN	Be quiet.

(comes and puts an arm around his shoulders)

Here, musician,

(as Joseph looks desperate)

drink this.

(offers him some juice that is on the bedside cabinet.)

JOSEPH   No no

(Benjamin still holds glass)

BENJAMIN   As I came in
here – a soft smell, licked
by carbolic

JOSEPH   It's always here.
BENJAMIN   But no gas.
Your ordeal, Gurney,
is finished.

JOSEPH   Just begun.   *(pause)*   Why 'Gurney', 'Gurney',
all the time?

BENJAMIN   I don't know you,
you feel alien to me.

JOSEPH   You make me feel mad,
drawing madness to the surface as a man draws water up
through the straw.   *(pause)*   See, you didn't have much
of a war, did you?

BENJAMIN   How could I? they gave me,
as you know, pure exemption.   *pause*
I've nothing more to
tell you now.   *(pause)*   Just your coldness.

JOSEPH   Not coldness,
a warmth, a pure caring for
myself.

BENJAMIN   Tomorrow, then.

(goading)

The gas terror will have worn away, perhaps

JOSEPH   the mists, the green misty dabs, – all away;
the phosgene, its coughs and froth. What
it does to a man, to many men

(Benjamin exits)

(shouts)   fuck off,

Critchley.

                    If only I could get out
of asylum; hospital
is clink.   *pause*
She, she, said I would mend. And she is good.
My best Gloucester's badge-of-the-line,
twined for her to a broach –
seen battle, seen courage, or the need for it: seen mud.
No need for that. I live in a tenement
these days, where the brain fumes.

Dusk. Enter Jenny.

JENNY   You are lucky to have
               a room to yourself, do you know?

                                        Silence

JOSEPH   Jenny.

JENNY   *(evading him)*

               A poet ought to know more
               than others do.

JOSEPH   Space, gratitude.
JENNY   Not enough.
               It's not just space, but privilege;
               a space on your own.

JOSEPH   Jenny.

JENNY   *(drawing blinds)*

               And light, here.   *(pause)*   But now, I come
               between you and that light.

JOSEPH   Come,
               please, with your dark.

JENNY   Dark? I must leave then.

JOSEPH   No Jenny.

JENNY   *(mimicking)*

                    No, Jenny.   *(pause)*   My name sounds
               strange in my mouth. Now I must sponge you;
               don't move Joseph.

               (pulls back bedclothes, starts to sponge him)

JOSEPH   When you do this to me, feelings
             inside me change.
             I feel clean, and the cleanness inside me
             impure.

JENNY   I could creddle you
             like a huge child.

JOSEPH   I've sent my Gloucester's badge

JENNY   lie down

JOSEPH   regimental badge – to be burned, softened and twined to make
             a broach for you.

JENNY   Thanks.

JOSEPH   No more
             than that? It's a pledge to you

JENNY   please
             lie down.   *(pause)*   *(looks at him)*   there are many ways
             to pledge.

JOSEPH   What do you mean?   *pause*
             Shall I kiss you Jenny.   *(kisses her)*   We are
             pledged sweethearts
             fused in brass, the lips
             upon their kiss.

JENNY   Yes, a kiss.
             And then, another kiss.
             Joseph, think of the spaces
             a person possesses. Me, for instance, one,
             such as a seal upon a child; but that's not it.
             Or in the hands cupped for water, but that
             is not it, either.

JOSEPH   Jenny

JENNY   not yet, Joseph.   *(pause)*   The space
             of hands in prayer, in which there's no space,
             which useful anguish keeps clasped.

JOSEPH   Jenny, kiss me.

JENNY   And space where the tongue rustles
             and another's invades.
             The moistening of speech. That's space, Joseph.

JOSEPH	Jenny I desire you.
JENNY	In War, space is absence; and perhaps a longer space than that.
JOSEPH	Jenny my badge is my seal.

(She takes his hand and puts it on her breast)

JENNY	This is, in its way, a seal, your hand on me, my spaces filled.

(With a slow and trembling movement he puts his arms round her and kisses her. She puts her hand on his chest)

JENNY	Wait Joseph, please, a moment more; whatever you think you seal, this is the sort of care I think I have for you.
JOSEPH	Open the lock-gates, Jenny that the waters sift through their flood.

Lights down, then up. Joseph is in a wheel-chair being pushed by one of two orderlies to a different part of the hospital. The orderlies are dressed in white. The orderlies each speak in a lowered voice, Joseph does not.

SECOND	I didn't bargain for this.
FIRST	It's just a job.
SECOND	From one place to another.
JOSEPH	Where are you taking me?
SECOND	I wanted to be a nurse.
FIRST	*(laughing)* You are – a proper one.
SECOND	All over the country. *(pause)* Fuck it.
JOSEPH	Where are you taking me?
FIRST	From one room to another. *(they enter a room and stop)* Now we wait.

pause. Absolute silence

(Enter Doctor in white coat)

DOCTOR	Good morning Gurney.
JOSEPH	Doctor –
DOCTOR	*(cutting Joseph off)* strap him to the chair.

Make sure he's properly restrained:

(They strap him to the chair carefully, so as not to mark him)

the arms out...the sleeves rolled;
and the feet bared.

(They do this)

Gurney, your nurse is off today.

JOSEPH	My nurse?
DOCTOR	*Your* nurse? You're still in the Army.
JOSEPH	Yes.
DOCTOR	Yes, Sir. *(pause)* Sir.
JOSEPH	This isn't England's Army.

(orderlies laugh)

DOCTOR	The door's shut.
JOSEPH	Oh, but it's comic.
DOCTOR	Just so
JOSEPH	as if the door had never been.

(First orderly moves menacingly towards Joseph, but Doctor indicates he does not wish this.)

DOCTOR	We continue our examination.

(smiling)

White skin.

JOSEPH	Muddy.
DOCTOR	*(sleek with inquiry)*

Gurney?

    silence

The problem is
I know the imperative of duty: you don't.
Are you still suffering the effects of gas?

    silence

79

What are the symptoms?

JOSEPH   Indigestion.

DOCTOR   We will take away that suffering.

JOSEPH   I swallowed gas
at the Third Somme: Passchendaele they call it.
I was England's soldier.

(the orderlies exchange glances)

DOCTOR   But weren't we, each, her soldiers?

JOSEPH   *(looking directly at each of them in turn)*

                                 All?
Shouldn't think so: no.

(the orderlies and doctor look displeased by this)

DOCTOR   Do you smoke?

                        silence

(Offers him a cigarette. Joseph shakes his head)

Are you prepared for further service
at the Front?   *(pause)*   Are you sick?
Stomach trouble from gas
is claimed. But Gurney, sickness, in war
as in peace, is cowardice. Or so we think
in England's England. We think...in War, nothing
so becomes a man as courage; nothing
so disfigures, as its lack. Therefore we think
to drive fear with fear away. Compris?

                        silence

Do you?   *(pause)*   We will make you afraid
of your fear.

*(Doctor nods to orderlies. One of them takes out a cigarette and
lights it. Offers it to Joseph, who shakes his head)*

               Woodbine. The sweetest small
cigarette. It's got lungs, see...

(he lights up and inhales)

when one smokes, mortar, shell, splinter,
seem as nothing

               (offers to Joseph)

won't you?

(Joseph shakes his head)   Right

then.

JOSEPH   *(panicking)*

I will burn: fire and skin. Ah!

They burn him with their cigarettes. He screams. Lights down.

Lights up. Back in previous room two mornings later. Joseph sits on the bed alternately still and restless. Sunlight in the white room gives it a merciless feel. Jenny enters briskly, glad to see him.

JENNY   I've been off two days, a soldier's week-end;
the next time, I'll take you out.   *(pause)*   Where is
the jug for washing you?   *Looks at him*
You feel shut-up, like a sweet-shop at nighttime.

JOSEPH   I've been given a new rank...in England's army

(Jenny notices burns on his arm)

JENNY   *(almost hysterical)*

what are they? I never saw those

JOSEPH   are
they...rancid?

JENNY   Rancid? How can they be? How,
Joseph? How did you get these?

(examines them, taking his arm)

JOSEPH   I feel...
when I touch them,
they're soft, gas-like – pure
carboniferous burn

JENNY   Joseph!

JOSEPH   and lain on
by the neurasthenic body, result:
putrescence.

JENNY   They're burns; cindery almost,
not putrescent. Ah, Joseph.

(she puts her arms round him)

JOSEPH   Love me?

JENNY   Your body is beautiful to me. You spoke
of me as a hidden flame, but you
are the evident one. I touch you: we are both
in great affection.   *(pause)*   Precious
light that I hug to me
like a milkmaid, as I once was, when
as a child I worked on our farm;
your unmuddied body, clear as milk,
yet milk that flows muscle

JOSEPH   constant even heat, from
a packet of wild flowers. Wild woodbine,
grave punitive flowers.

JENNY   *(grasping his hands)*

                          I've got you Joseph

JOSEPH   Green ochreous gas, mists that chew the lungs: of that
I'd less than my fellows – the least, in truth.
I'm not bad, that's a fact. Though gassed,
I didn't burn...burned for
being not gassed enough. The wet meadows of blood toss
the reflected body malingering between
France and Gloucester. If you've had enough,
get away with you, England says, you–
unappealing to God,
a little wet dribble of self.

JENNY   Hold my
hands, you're cold.

*He does so. Knock at the door. Sufficient pause to let Benjamin enter without his
offering offence. Jenny gets Joseph into bed and covers his arms with sheet. Benjamin
enters, with books of music.*

BENJAMIN   *(to Jenny)* Good morning, ma'am. *(to Joseph)* Have you seen
Vaughan Williams' new songs?

JENNY   I think Joseph
is still unwell

BENJAMIN   though this might cheer him.
And the man might be Joseph's tutor, if Joseph
returns to the Academy.

JENNY	He will.
BENJAMIN	Then this is for him. *(offers Joseph the music)*
JENNY	Joseph needs rest not music.
BENJAMIN	Ma'am, with due respect, but Joseph needs rest and music.
JOSEPH	Benjamin, this huge fly and a compact ladybird rest on a leaf. They are not friends, they have not to do with each other.

(Jenny looks at him but before she is able to stop him he has twitched the sheet off and shows his burns)

Isn't this a beauty?

BENJAMIN	Beauties they are!
JENNY	You ought to leave Private Gurney to the care of the Hospital.
BENJAMIN	I say I beg to doubt that. *(pause)* *(deferentially)* May I talk with Joseph? My right as a friend.
JENNY	*(hesitating)* For a while. Joseph still needs rest.

(Jenny exits)

BENJAMIN	What's been done to you?

silence

Your songs, your good verse, your love, that at least.

JOSEPH	Don't want them. I've no honour: shame and burns.

(lifts up arm and again rolls up pyjama sleeve)

Am I then disgraced?

BENJAMIN	Not disgraced, shamed; as wounds shame.
	(moves as before to put his arms round Joseph)
JOSEPH	You keep away from me. *(pause)* Went through my skin with a wild woodbine, flowering of a sorts. Dark buttery flowers.
	I've shut the lock-gates. The sheets of water shan't get through – laminate on each other, arctic, the moon's integument, awful – the abode of madness, Benjamin.
BENJAMIN	You make me feel as you do.
JOSEPH	*(laughing)* No. *(pause)* Not like me. *(pause)* And so, do you love my music? Or shall I stop my music?
BENJAMIN	How can I answer that?
JOSEPH	Very easily. *(pause)* I malinger in the department of the head, in every department, if you want to know. *pause* Would you do me a favour.
BENJAMIN	What favour?
JOSEPH	I am serious. Do you have a sharp blade?
BENJAMIN	I care deeply for your music.
JOSEPH	Yes...
BENJAMIN	a blade...
JOSEPH	yes *pause*
BENJAMIN	meaning, "sharp"?
JOSEPH	adequate to cut threads...spidery filaments from each stalk... in my field that was a muddy emerald
BENJAMIN	what for?

JOSEPH   *(wearily, as if to a child)*
                        I have told you. I want
              to be killed; I want
              an expanse of meadow, peaceable and unashamed.
              I want extinction, into a new life.
              Only cowardice prevents

BENJAMIN   Give me the reasons, first,
              why I should –

JOSEPH   because I need to die.
              and even that is incorrect: I want
              to be killed

BENJAMIN   Reason?

JOSEPH   My friend with
              a talent for order should "not find
              that strange". You don't happen
              to possess a knife, do you?

BENJAMIN   You find one.

JOSEPH   Because there are,
              here, all manner of surgical knifes,
              but hard to nick one

BENJAMIN   leave me be

JOSEPH   *(laughing)*

              Oh, that's it. A friend in need indeed. How
              shall I leave here?   *(pause)*   You are
              as much a coward as me.   *(pause)*   Kill me, musician;
              then each of us has no shame.

              (Benjamin produces from his pocket a quite substantial pocket-knife. Holds it out to Joseph)

BENJAMIN   You do it.

JOSEPH   When I was twelve
              I put a marble in my mouth; if I
              could swallow it and die, I was insane.
              But if I left it balancing on my tongue
              then I was mad to put it there.

              (takes knife from Benjamin)

85

Is this the very
thing we are waiting for?

*(Enter Jenny, without knocking, with a Hospital Doctor. Joseph
conceals knife calmly.)*

DOCTOR   *(to Benjamin)*   I think you must
leave now. Our patient seems taxed enough.

BENJAMIN   Yes.

Act 4, scene 2

Joseph alone. Hymn, 'I vow to thee my country', in the background.

JOSEPH   If I'm incurable, and suffer like any person
may; if I'm mad, why must I hurt
and be mad, when only the whole and sane
hurt, who know and feel their pain?
Madness often obliterates: it should do.
It should obliterate pain.

Act 4, scene 3

*Barnwood House, a mental institution on the outskirts of Gloucester. A large house,
and, in a sizeable front-room, a big window, the top of which shapes like a brace
(bracket). This part has stained glass; the remainder, which is large, has only vertical
and horizontal mullions. A large clock, also resembling a brace, as if mimicking the
top part of the window, ticks on the mantle-shelf. December evening, 1918. The War
is over. Joseph is with his mother and Canon Cheesman. Mrs. Gurney appears older.*

FLORENCE   Ten shilling. *(She offers Joseph a note; he accepts)*
                    And a tin of tobacco; you asked me
but after this, no more.

(Joseph pushes away tin. His mother returns it to her shopping-bag)

CHEESMAN   Oh, gentle Joseph.

                    pause.   *Fishes in his pocket*

Here's another ten shilling.

FLORENCE   No.

CHEESMAN   *(to Florence)*

Please; if one has nothing else,
one may have money.

(Joseph holds out his hand)

86

FLORENCE	Joseph!
JOSEPH	I would rathr die in great pain –
	(Joseph takes note) than suffer
	her generosity.
CHEESMAN	Joseph,
	we do not speak of pain.
FLORENCE	You are too gentle
	by half, Canon Cheesman.

(Joseph gets up and walks to the clock, stares at it, turns to face his mother)

And I dislike how you get it wrong,
or you forget what you don't care about; *(pause)* it was
my birthday, five days back.

CHEESMAN	There's still time to remember, Mrs Gurney.
JOSEPH	No; with mother, there's no memory,
	only a harsh space, inhospitable geography.

pause

I hope father's comfortable now.

FLORENCE	Wicked.
JOSEPH	*(to Cheesman; confidential, cheerful)*
	Father's dead
	you know.
	(to Florence)
	Best place for him, I should think.

pause

Just pray he's comfortable.
Plenty of soldiers fastened by mud
weren't, in such a death.

FLORENCE	*(stammering, close to tears)*
	Shut you mouth.
JOSEPH	My mouth? is
	that all?
	(to Cheesman)

<pre>
                    Several years back, father
            died; I haven't even forgotten.
            And she's complaining for she thinks
            I default five days on her birthday.

                                        pause
CHEESMAN   (gently putting his hand on Joseph's arm)

            Enough, Joseph,
            my dear child.

FLORENCE   No son of yours. Though
            after your fashion, he might be.

CHEESMAN   I beg you, Mrs Gurney,
            to forgive me; I meant no harm.

FLORENCE   And managed none.   (pause)   What
            is to be done – a son, like a stray,
            in the family of us Luggs? Never before

JOSEPH   have me put down,
            that's best.

FLORENCE   I had you. I suffered you.

JOSEPH   You needn't have
            but for an error in the flesh

FLORENCE   you tat,
            you bit of flea

JOSEPH   I asked nothing,
            then, of you. My father asked,
            and was suffered.

FLORENCE   You'd better not been born

JOSEPH   I feel that,
            as if I'd never been.
            But since I live – I'll tell you mother,
            I'm to survive –
            nor you shan't stand before me!

FLORENCE   Your madness
            may. Consider that.

CHEESMAN   He is ill,
            Mrs Gurney, not mad. Never
            say it.
</pre>

FLORENCE	I do say. Never
	a Lugg, but a Gurney.
	A true Gurney, and passing onwards
	into more. *pause* *To Joseph*
	So you receive
	tobacco, an' you forget. An' as for cash,
	the memory don't linger, do it?
JOSEPH	*(correcting her)*
	Does it. *(pause)* They gave me burns
FLORENCE	And I wish you'd not invent
	what no one would ever in – where
	are they, the burns?
JOSEPH	the wildest woodbines,
	Mother, like the forest flowers, fade.
CHEESMAN	Jean Elliot's
	lament for the Scottish dead at Flodden Field.
	pause
	Mrs Gurney, your son
	is ill: needs kindness. Clearly.
FLORENCE	*(to Joseph)*
	Easier to be the way
	you are, than stay...sane,
	stable, upright. Like them flowers
	in the field.
JOSEPH	Oh, you heard that?
FLORENCE	easier
	to be how you are, than stay sane.
	The huge Cathedral
	towers upright. Why not you?
	Son of the Cathedral, son of the Luggs. We all suffer,
	all get pained.
JOSEPH	Ma'am!
	we either bear or break.
FLORENCE	Don't, then.

CHEESMAN   Florence, mother to my godchild.

             (Florence stares at Cheesman)

FLORENCE   *(to Joseph)*   To be burned. That's
             a price the soldier bears with. Though I doubt
             you were.

JOSEPH   Doubt it, mother?

FLORENCE   Yes,
             doubt it.

JOSEPH   And I doubt you will suffer
             me the price of some tobacco.

FLORENCE   *(going through shopping-bag until she finds, and hands him, the tin
             of tobacco)*
             We all must suffer, all stay whole.

JOSEPH   It's what you say.

FLORENCE   And you destroy
             all I say.

                                       pause

JOSEPH   Mother, need we
             wrangle?

FLORENCE   We need not.

                                       pause

JOSEPH   I want to leave now. Help me.

FLORENCE   Leave? not likely. Pain leaks responsibility.
             Remember what you were at home? You stay.

*Knock at the door, and enter the Director of the Institution, a middle-aged man – thin
legs, quite well-knit body with a paunch beginning to develop, and with a
disproportionately large head. The face is austere, yet humorous and kindly –
something like the face of John Clare.*

DIRECTOR   *(to Joseph)*

             A friend from London has arrived, and is anxious to speak with you –
             she has received your letter, and, as you may think, is upset.
             Will you spare her the time?   *(pause)*   You are alive, despite all,
             and we are glad. May Elizabeth come to you?

JOSEPH   She may.

90

	(exit Director)
CHEESMAN	No more than that, no more moist a greeting than – she, your friend, may?
FLORENCE	*(preparing to leave)* You were never a warm friend.
JOSEPH	As you say, mother; as you have said. It's all one to me.

(Florence approaches him. Stands before him, then abruptly slaps his face)

JOSEPH	You've been wanting to do that for a few years.
FLORENCE	*(with dignity)* Better than that: I've done it.

(Florence exits. Long pause)

JOSEPH	I hate my cold mother who loved neither my father's gentle useless body, nor her milk she fed me with.

Cheesman comes up and puts his arms round him decorously. There is a deep, grave affection. A knock. Pause. Another knock.

CHEESMAN	*(as Elizabeth enters)* Joseph.
JOSEPH	The fat cumulus is in the still blue, and a darkness...*(stammers)*...in...in...inheres in everything.
CHEESMAN	Force no tears from me, I pray you.
JOSEPH	No. *pause* I don't want to depend upon a soul, who have none myself. *(pause)* Give me back dignity.
CHEESMAN	*(despairing)* Is that why you enlisted?
JOSEPH	Why? to kill myself? you're hopeful, aren't you?

(they stare at each other)

CHEESMAN   I'll leave you just now.
            (exit Cheesman)
JOSEPH   *(to himself)*
            What's in it for me, who served
            England? Soldier, writer, musician...patriot
            to Gloucester's meadows; ah, no, its lawns, its trim
            trimmed awful respectability.
            God, am I now
            to hate what I love, as much as I hate me?

ELIZABETH   Your letter came through.   *(pause)*   I know; *(Takes his
                                                        hands)* Beethoven
            spoke to you, *(Joseph nods)* but was reluctant
            to say much of Benjamin. What did you reply?   *pause*
            'How I would like to see your face', you wrote.
            You see it now.   *(pause)*   You needn't speak, though.

                                pause

            Oh my love. *(Takes his hands and kisses them. Joseph recoils.)*
                                                                    what!
            What is it? do we speak in unbidden language!
            show me, Joseph, the coat of colours, promise
            given once
JOSEPH   once refused.
ELIZABETH   Not
            true.

JOSEPH   No.   *(pause)*   Nor am I Joseph, deft
            in a single item.

ELIZABETH   Deft?
            who has the badge to be melted into
            a broach – who was that for?

JOSEPH   The business of love
            is to strike into another's feelings.   *pause*
            I'm in the bin, serving England: one of her soldiers.
            'We are England'...

ELIZABETH   and what are we
            who remained in England?

92

JOSEPH   The not-England we served. I shall
            die here; I'm mad,
            and so I conclude I must
            bury myself here. Decent Elizaeth,
            twined onto my badge, in a way,
            making a good broach. I'm sorry, sorry
            for my being...

ELIZABETH   so what will
            you do?

JOSEPH   Do?   *(pause)*   The act of tupping.
            Better, I think, than I did.

ELIZABETH   Joseph, you will
            heal, the coat be dipped in many colours –
            everyone shall see.

JOSEPH   England looks like a pig
            that sits up, begging. It begged my life,
            and now has no use for it.
            Nor have I. I tried
            killing myself. As you know. Didn't work. Volumes
            of water held behind jammed lock-gates,
            though it ached and bulged, an eyeball
            sweating, exasperated,
            in the gas. And which got me for I swallowed some,
            not hardly enough...
            Chlorina-phosgena, daughter of war. Fine sight,
            we, in your misty powers.

ELIZABETH   Tell me nothing more.

JOSEPH   You suspect
            me of something.

ELIZABETH   I am certain.   *pause*

            Joseph,
            come whole, leave this place.

JOSEPH   I want
            what they say love is: the badge
            with love twined in
            its arms, brave insignia

ELIZABETH	you've already given that away.
JOSEPH	Did you know they tortured me in hospital?
ELIZABETH	True?
JOSEPH	Burned me. But now the flowers are healed. I screamed and screamed. No water could save or heal me. The pain saved me. I saved me.
ELIZABETH	Yes, love, you did, you will.
JOSEPH	Will you make love, sometime? A soldier might always die.
ELIZABETH	Love, Joseph, as someone else already has? Has already been where the twin eggs are in the nest in tufts of grass, its ruff of animal manners... hasn't someone?

silence

and rejected you?

silence

There are women like that.

silence

Now, especially. Who want the speckled eggs,
its natural stable meat, not what hatches from them.

silence

No warmth. Botched, all botched.

JOSEPH	Leave me, then. Get of this place. It's...the whole of... this room is mine.

(moving towards her)

94

ELIZABETH	No, I love you, I do love you, Joseph. It was a fit of envy for warmth exchanged with another.
JOSEPH	None loves me. Mother was supposed to visit! she did! It's hateful, love is hateful to me.
ELIZABETH	Let me touch you.
JOSEPH	It is all much too late. When I was a child I should have been touched. Was not. Abandon me. Prove me right. Do you have ten shilling to spare?
ELIZABETH	*(fumbling hastily in her bag)*

ELIZABETH
                                               I have
somewhere.

JOSEPH   Good.

Director knocks and enters

DIRECTOR   I heard some noise.

ELIZABETH   Here it is. *(gives him the note)*

DIRECTOR   You shouldn't
you know, Ma'am. He has to learn to live
away from the world, so as
to enter it again.

ELIZABETH   Oh, thank you.

(to Joseph)

I'll be back, tomorrow, early morning. I will
be back. Prove me, Joseph. And Benjamin will. We both
stay in the same Inn. *The Globe*, I think.
Your friends are gathering

(Goes to him, gives him a quick embrace and a kiss. Exit.)

DIRECTOR   I heard shouting.

JOSEPH   You did not, sir;
Gloucestershire never shouts.

                                        pause

95

DIRECTOR   I did
         though.   *(pause)*   You need not shout.
         Some of the world is not deaf
         though much of it seems so. Goodnight to you
         my friend.

         (Puts his hand on Joseph's arm, looks kindly at him and leaves)

JOSEPH   I will not...
         what is this egg of kindness to hatch
         me out, raw, a beaky flocculent chick?
         I will not stay,
         neither. They want to detain me
         for kindness' sake. They shan't sup,
         savour, or salt my musical company. The locusts.
         No, sir. Not.   *(pause)*   There is no Time.

Picks up clock, looks at window, and then hurls the clock at it. Shatters. Scrambles through and away

Act 4, scene 4

A traditional inn, of Jacobean age, in Gloucester. Same 24 hours, but later that night. Benjamin sits at table, writing his music. He appears to progress. He gets up, and hums, softly, but in a harsh, surprisingly unmusical voice, what he's been writing. Competent, well-made; takes no risks. Stable key, not enharmonic. Wanders round room. He is not in a state of pre-lyrical tension. After a while, gets up again, hums his work – then, he takes the manuscript in his hands and tears it up with deliberated, well-ordered, but pitiable aggression.

BENJAMIN   I shall be married soon. That is to be fruitful.
             To insert the fruit
             into the womb: joy thereof, as they say.   *pause*
             Music: a well-ordered aggression...
             I am not a fool. It's better than that, I know.
             I know – more than I do know, that's
             for sure. So, music is...feeling's challenge – its risk.   *pause*
             Harmony and disorder.
             Energy that must have order, energy that must not,
             to keep its energy. How can I do it?

                                    knock

             Yes.

             (enter Elizabeth)

ELIZABETH   I saw Joseph
this afternoon.

BENJAMIN   Yes.

ELIZABETH   When will you
go to him?

BENJAMIN   I don't know exactly.

ELIZABETH   You will
though?

                              pause

                  Benjamin, what is it?

BENJAMIN   Benjamin, what is it? Oh nothing, Benjamin.   *pause*
Is this the finish of Gurney?

ELIZABETH   An end to Joseph:
his life, or his works?

BENJAMIN   To the one
that gives each of us the most.

ELIZABETH   His life.

BENJAMIN   His songs: the rush of muddied, pure
water. Evidently
I too wish him to live

ELIZABETH   What would a friend want
for another?

BENJAMIN   You must ask yourself that.

ELIZABETH   Is there a life
without the works – that gilded insect?

BENJAMIN   Insect?

ELIZABETH   the life's works, frail, easily
disposed of. And once the smudge,
like lamp-black, on a sheet of empty paper –
once done with, then the life of a friend
is easily tolerated.

BENJAMIN   So you say

ELIZABETH   Yes, Benjamin, I do say.

BENJAMIN	Gurney is in love with you – as he says, love twined and true on a badge: as you know. Such a life would make the songs
ELIZABETH	You yourself make songs, I think; their golden fluted mouths are sharp and grinning. Oh, yes – music. But Gurney is lost.

(exit Elizabeth)

BENJAMIN	Gurney, your insignia is music; but that badge, sex, has taken you. You want what feeds love, but isn't love. *(pause)* Love *and* work. Yet if it's love without work, her's is an empty belly... love gushes into the space, but hugs a banal fruit... pulp, and slippery pip... quite simply, I am going to fail and die. If before that

(knock at door)

                    yes

(enter waiter)

WAITER	Late, sir. I'm late. In this place are many rooms.
BENJAMIN	Please put the wine there.
WAITER	Sir, of course. Have you seen the other ones – lacey wood, swarthy grain; and in each sits a thirsty man.
BENJAMIN	All right
WAITER	sir, a bottle of *Bull's Blood*, vintage with an iron taste, from Hungary.

(exit waiter)

BENJAMIN	The English are mad; I hope he doesn't poison me. *pause* I'm not Mozart, have no Salieri, poisoner to a careless, wasteful talent. I want fruition, the sexual luck to make me, enable me to touch another with my mind's music, harmonious

	energy. That's not it. I want to... That mad Gurney life takes my sane life, its gassed life for
	(knock at door, enter waiter with more wine)
WAITER	Sir, I could not prevent him...
	(Enter Joseph, breathless, dishevelled, and cheerful. He wears his pilot's jacket and a pink neckerchief)
JOSEPH	Hello, Benjamin.
	(takes bottle of wine off Waiter)
BENJAMIN	You out?
JOSEPH	Have you a handkerchief, I've cut myself.
	(shows him his cut hands)
BENJAMIN	Barnwood's Warden, that gentle man – has he paroled you?
JOSEPH	No. *(pause)* I threw a clock at that stained glass, and where a clearness got broken, I, gentle and quite dotty, broke through and climbed out, more prickly than trench wire. Madame, no bon. I suppose.
	(Benjamin hands him his handkerchief, and Joseph gravely binds his hand with it)
BENJAMIN	Bring more wine, in a few minutes.
WAITER	Sir.
	(exit Waiter)
JOSEPH	Does that devil deal in potions? Oh, tray bong.
BENJAMIN	Tomorrow, I was to come to you.
JOSEPH	Tomorrow, I am here, instead. How's your cage? Some of us die unpensioned with a hundred friends. Pass the wine, please.
	(Benjamin hesitates, then passes him the bottle)
	(reads)
	'Bull's Blood'. How many for how much concentrate of blood?

	The blood of sacrifice, soldier's blood,
	yields a cup-full.
	Oh we are a religious lot, we 'men'.
BENJAMIN	Now this war's ended, what will you do?
JOSEPH	I'd like
	to marry, like you. If I'm mad enough
	they'll allow it, I should think.

BENJAMIN   But for work?

JOSEPH   They say, jobs, as never before.
I'd sell garters, matches, or my quick body
to a rich, handy widow. Or pluck
insurance off the needy.

BENJAMIN   We need
music from you, even if it destroys you.

JOSEPH   Destroys me? What does that mean to you?
You had no war, just a fiancée...
war music, war poetry, war
and its sweat – the oxidation of larches in a wood.
I am a war poet.

                                            pause

You'll bring me fruit, and inquire
about my soul, as the man says.

BENJAMIN   Jenny?

JOSEPH   What's she to you? She loves me, she doesn't love me.
She wants a simple untalented jock,
not one like me. Gloucestershire hill, cottage
of stone and wood, in it a jar. –
Put in your pennies, chink, – there they go
no, she don't

BENJAMIN   two weeks ago she loved you.
In Edinburgh.

JOSEPH   She don't like gas

BENJAMIN   you're through it now

JOSEPH   in my spare time I am. I'll be married...
I want to fuck, that's the hunger;
I learned it in the army. I want the fragile wrists
pressing the back of my neck,

100

	fragile and gleaming...
	I also like men. And when I watched them,
	manly men, in the army, so much muscle and unconcerned psyche
	in the trenches, afraid of death –
	that's how I wish I was,
	a workman
BENJAMIN	you're a musician, with talent
JOSEPH	I'm a wangler, scorched me with fags...
	you don't happen to have a revolver do you?
	see, Benjamin,
	I give you permission to destroy me.
	I can't say fairer than that
BENJAMIN	you need a job,
	if you come out of the asylum
JOSEPH	absolutely correct.

If. You're correct, and I'm evasive. Perhaps
I'd play interval music in a cinema
or for a silent film. In the army
death distracted a good many. We grew
scruff and lice, but delivered the creatures
to a candle: phut, they were gone. The flesh sputtered...
or was made jagged, as if the bowels
had given way with a cancer.
An arm was stuck in the mud, help me, it said.
Permit me, sir, I said, to crawl through.
No Gurney, he said, certain death, that.
So I didn't. Next time, after you, sir, I said,   *pause*
and he crawled through and died.
If I could put my music together
I would, with another's words against
my blither, my solid thudding jars of noise,
in a cottage at Maisemore.
Two pink eaved windows, pink as the dugs of a sow.
The sow farrowed, and I helped her. Benjamin, it was the closest
I came to maternity – to creation.
The moon delicate as milk, as grated cheese,
sifts through leaves – I think they're sycamore.
Look at that tree

(goes to window)

	it shakes with rooks
	(Benjamin comes over with him)
	it's large leaves, smudgy in the breeze.
BENJAMIN	I wonder, Joseph, you don't go home.
JOSEPH	where? large birds
	like pendulums, shaking.
	Flutter with love, they do.
BENJAMIN	They are leaves
JOSEPH	vibrate, twitch, jerk their fantails
	with love, I suppose
BENJAMIN	they're not birds
JOSEPH	ah, well, they are birds.
BENJAMIN	It's as if you had two selves.
	In you, the fresh-water surface holds
	two persons – a coat lined double.
	You rip its lining
	away, the other holds the coat
	even closer. If one self creates
	and suffers, the other cares
	for self with a small, even, devouring
	appetite. It weeps for gratification.
	Joseph, Elizabeth is leaving you –
JOSEPH	Even war
	gets up and leaves. What can you know
	of this quick-footed movement
	of leaving, its timid flustered creature?
	The republic of failure
	aches...Madame, no bon.
	(Knock. Enter Waitress with roast meat and carvers, Waiter with the wine.)
WAITRESS	A little meat, sirs. I made the meat,
	and the men made the War. *pause*
	Please to carve for yourselves.
BENJAMIN	Put it down...somewhere.
WAITRESS	*(to Benjamin)* Will you?

(Looks at Joseph quickly. Joseph turns to look at her.)

Or perhaps your gentleman friend will.   *pause*

BENJAMIN   Either will do.

WAITER   Sir, I have something
to recommend.

BENJAMIN   Nothing else...we...I:
nothing more.

JOSEPH   What's on offer?

WAITER   Sir,
sorts of post-war dallying.
Sailor's tabernacle, corrugated iron and a psalm.

(pours wine and offers it, first to Benjamin, then to Joseph)

(to Joseph)

You're from here?

(exit Waitress)

JOSEPH   Sort of.

WAITER   Been born here,
soldier?

JOSEPH   Soldier!

WAITER   behind the stairs,
prosperous bodies. Oh, lush. And now, sir,
I could show you – in this inn
of several rooms, each hinges is
different. And in each room

BENJAMIN   I don't want to hear

JOSEPH   For it is better to marry than to burn.

WAITER   Is the gentlemen to be married soon?
you must train first, to be married. It's no use
putting your tongue to the furrow an' you don't know
how tongue and plow is together,
the horse is known for what it is

BENJAMIN   out – get out!

WAITER   Sir, I will.

JOSEPH	But Benjamin, I like this.
BENJAMIN	The war has done you no good
JOSEPH	you are right. The peace must mend me.
WAITER	It must. None of the nun's habit, but dark stockings a band of white at her thighs.
BENJAMIN	This room at least is not your brothel.
WAITER	Right sir.
JOSEPH	It's a room for allsorts, the snips of envy that unhang a man's muscle
WAITER	the Welsh bring their girls to their knees here
BENJAMIN	*(to Joseph)*　envy! no envy! Yours is the talent.
JOSEPH	Ah, it was, it might-have-been. The mind unhinges like an elbow bending the wrong way – a cat's. Let's see the white thighs stood before a Jacobean fireplace – all mermaidens, fishes, escutcheon: gold, green, brass and blue.
BENJAMIN	But this isn't love
JOSEPH	damned right
WAITER	but can lead to it, sir, loosens the arrow, moistens the tip, may bring one to love.
BENJAMIN	*(pushing Waiter towards the door)* Bring more wine. *(follows Waiter towards door and speaks quietly but urgently to him)* My friend has escaped from the asylum. He must be returned.

WAITER   *(for Joseph, but looking straight at Benjamin)*
                I shall bring that lady up
                (exit Waiter)
BENJAMIN   What are you doing?
                You need love, not sex
JOSEPH   I have sex
                and want more. Love I cannot have.

                pause

                But you have love and I'm glad for you.

A knock. Enter waitress but without her uniform. Waiter enters with her. We see her more clearly now. She has a good figure, but her face is middle-aged, raddled somewhat, and unhappy. She is dressed in black, thin woolen stockings, and her thighs, which are strong and elegant, have an exposed white flesh part, between stockings and pants. Her shoulders are erect, still, and slim. Her arms long, but the skin round the elbows is a bit wrinkled. She enters slightly unsteady. Her voice entirely in control. She is Welsh. Dignified contralto.

WAITER   *(pointing to Joseph)*
                That's your man, he's the one
JOSEPH   *(with compassion)*
                Oh, for the love of God.
WAITRESS   *(calmly)*
                                 No, not he.
WAITER   *(to waitress)*
                Is he not?

She hesitates, goes to him and, calmly again, puts an arm around his neck, draws him to her and kisses him. Not passionate, but merciful, and winsome.

WAITRESS   Any luck, soldier?
WAITER   *(to Benjamin)*
                This, sir, is the feast of Saint Stephen's. Each day,
                above the jewellers next door, figures
                of a Welsh woman in witches hat, dairymaid,
                kilted soldier and a gilt Father Time, strike
                bells in Gloucester to signify
                how penury, grime, sickness, the deceits

of small-print insurance are set aside – so we enjoy
a bit of feast at each year's end.   *pause*
Move on, sir, enjoy wine and meat.

(Exit Waiter)

WAITRESS   *(to Joseph)*

You've not much time have you?

JOSEPH   *pause*

I hope I may have. What else have I?

WAITRESS   My body is still good.
And I know the soldier's hunger can't be
relieved – that his spunk,
his shooting out is no relief...

BENJAMIN   *(going up to her and almost striking her)*

you –

you disgust me.

JOSEPH   *(taking hold of Benjamin's hand so that he can't strike her)*

But not me, she don't.
You: stick to your marriage, Critchley;
each to what he can manage.

WAITRESS   *(to Benjamin)*

My time, sir, is your friend's pleasure.

JOSEPH   *(to Waitress)*

Where may I find you?

(during this time Benjamin makes efforts to disengage himself but Joseph's grip is too strong)

WAITRESS   a room tucked in
by the empty billiard-hall – friend
touch me as if I were your child.

(she goes to Joseph and touches his hand. Exits.)

BENJAMIN   I think you can release me.

(Joseph releases him)

JOSEPH   You make me think I don't want
to be an intellectual.

BENJAMIN	Oh yes? *pause* Animal! Mozart! Profligate talent!
JOSEPH	You, Salieri! *(pause)* That's About evens.

silence

	You disgust me though. I'd rather be a lock-keeper, than a man with just a brain. Stab, stab – the brain. And that's all, on its own, it amounts to
BENJAMIN	with your talent! Is that all you want with it? Lock-keeper of foul water. You make me feel unclean.
JOSEPH	You've done that, you've made a suppuration of your self. A canker in place of our friendship
BENJAMIN	– at least you will not – fuck – as you call it.
JOSEPH	But you'll – fuck – your wife. If you don't, you'll be stinking fish to her.

(Joseph goes as if to leave)

BENJAMIN	You're not leaving yet.
JOSEPH	I am.
BENJAMIN	You're going back to the institution, returned to the quiet house, with a good man.
JOSEPH	You want that, don't you? *(pause)* who's to assist you? I'm leaving.
BENJAMIN	No.

Joseph moves towards door. Benjamin tries to block him. Joseph pushes him out of the way. Benjamin picks up the carving knife and with it blocks Joseph's exit. Joseph retaliates, taking hold of the hand of Benjamin's that holds the knife. Then Joseph slowly turns it towards Benjamin.

JOSEPH	I am the King in the wheat fields. You're the corn-dolly amongst the husks and shredded ears. One of us must leave, Benjamin – Now

With a sudden thrust he pushes Benjamin's hand with the knife so that it then slowly but firmly enters Benjamin. They stare at each other as Joseph does this. Then Joseph stands, holding his hands down by his side, staring at Benjamin dead. Waiter shows himself in doorway.

WAITER   You were sudden: I was a bit late.   *pause*
                     You will need to return. *(nodding)* I'm sure.   *pause*
                     Better the small prickly
                     lane to Barnwood,
                     than the wide hung road. Be made
                     by the occasion.

JOSEPH   How shall I be made?   *pause*
                     The reformatory, the men's boy's
                     prison for the mad. I killed him
                     – like I killed in the army.

WAITER   I saw nothing. Not a thing.
                     Justice and quietness.

JOSEPH   Justice,
                     not quietness.

(END)